AF579318

The Grand Trunk Road

Khyber to Calcutta

The Grand Trunk Road

Khyber to Calcutta

JOHN WILES

Elek London

Published in Great Britain by
Paul Elek Books Limited
54-58 Caledonian Road, London N1 9RN

ISBN 0 236 15445

Made and printed in Great Britain
at the St. Ann's Press, Park Road, Altrincham, Cheshire, WA14 5QQ

The unit of currency in Pakistan and India is the rupee, which is subdivided into 100 paise. At the time of my journey the Pakistani rupee was worth just over 8p. The Indian rupee was worth about 5½p. Prior to decimalization the rupee in Pakistan and India was divided into 16 annas and prices in these countries are still frequently expressed in annas though payment is made in the new coinage.

List of Plates

The photographs were taken by the author

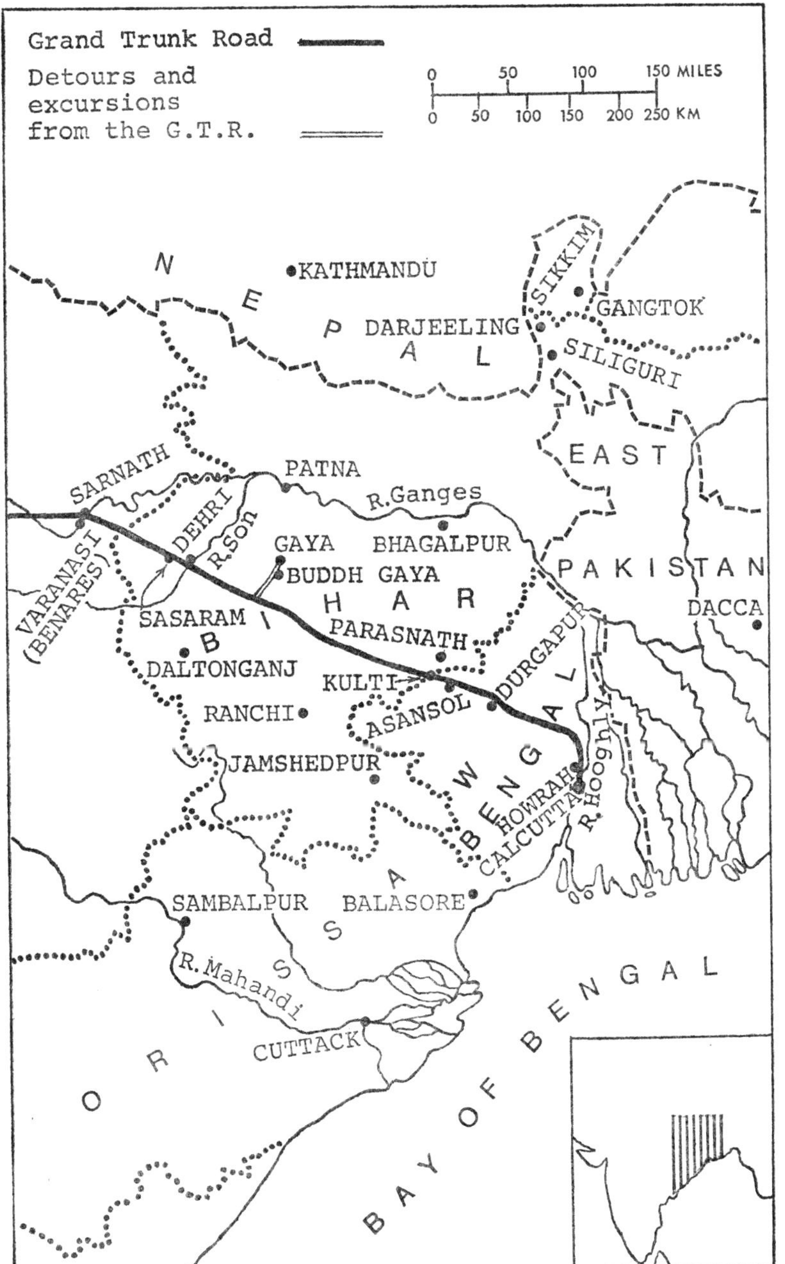

Grand Trunk Road
Detours and excursions from the G.T.R.
0 50 100 150 MILES
0 50 100 150 200 250 KM
NEPAL
KATHMANDU
SIKKIM
GANGTOK
DARJEELING
SILIGURI
EAST PAKISTAN
DACCA
SARNATH
PATNA
R.Ganges
DEHRI
R.Son
GAYA
BHAGALPUR
BUDDH GAYA
VARANASI (BENARES)
SASARAM
BIHAR
PARASNATH
DALTONGANJ
KULTI
DURGAPUR
ASANSOL
RANCHI
JAMSHEDPUR
WEST BENGAL
HOWRAH
CALCUTTA
R.Hooghly
SAMBALPUR
BALASORE
ORISSA
R.Mahandi
CUTTACK
BAY OF BENGAL

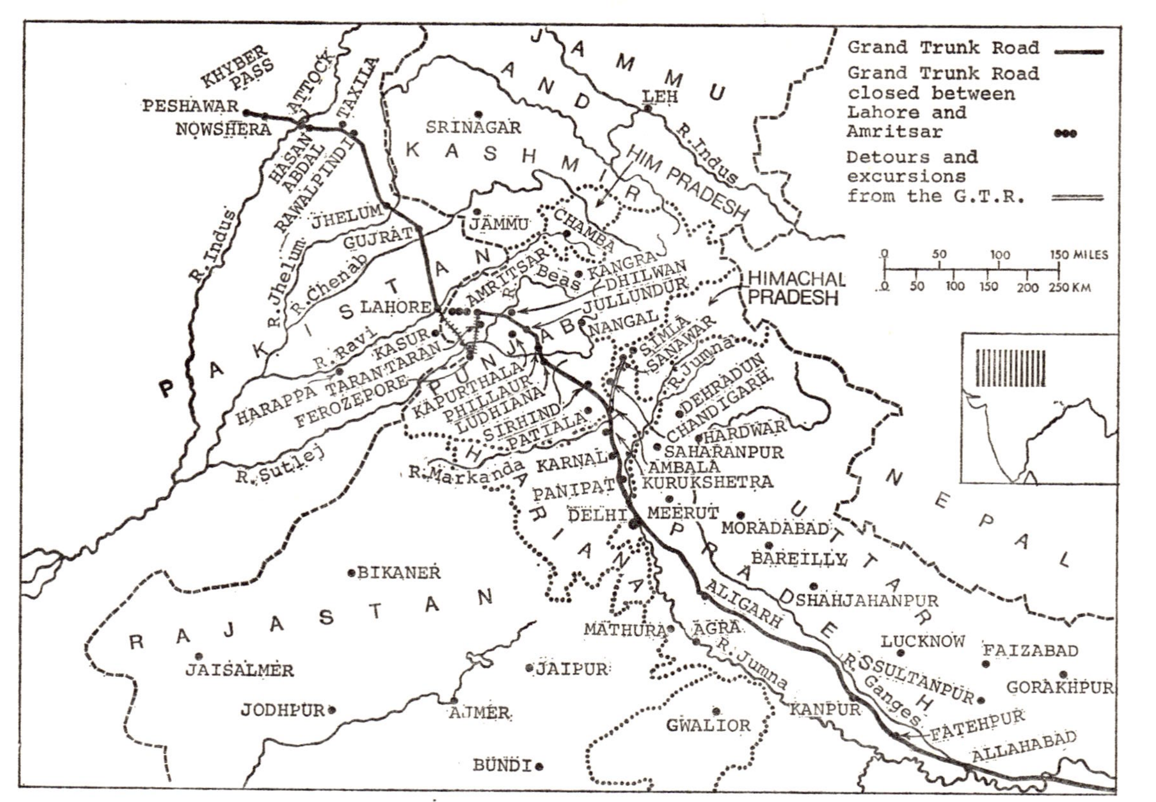

Grand Trunk Road
Grand Trunk Road closed between Lahore and Amritsar
Detours and excursions from the G.T.R.
0 50 100 150 MILES
0 50 100 150 200 250 KM
KHYBER PASS
PESHAWAR
NOWSHERA
ATTOCK
HASAN ABDAL
TAXILA
RAWALPINDI
JHELUM
GUJRAT
R. Indus
R. Jhelum
R. Chenab
R. Ravi
R. Beas
R. Sutlej
R. Markanda
R. Jumna
R. Ganges
JAMMU AND KASHMIR
SRINAGAR
LEH
JAMMU
HIM PRADESH
HIMACHAL PRADESH
CHAMBA
KANGRA
DHILWAN
JULLUNDUR
NANGAL
SIMLA
SANAWAR
PAKISTAN
LAHORE
AMRITSAR
KASUR
TARAN TARAN
HARAPPA
FEROZEPORE
PUNJAB
KAPURTHALA
PHILLAUR
LUDHIANA
SIRHIND
PATIALA
HARIANA
KARNAL
PANIPAT
DELHI
AMBALA
KURUKSHETRA
DEHRADUN
CHANDIGARH
HARDWAR
SAHARANPUR
MEERUT
MORADABAD
BAREILLY
SHAHJAHANPUR
UTTAR PRADESH
NEPAL
ALIGARH
MATHURA
AGRA
LUCKNOW
FAIZABAD
GORAKHPUR
SULTANPUR
KANPUR
FATEHPUR
ALLAHABAD
RAJASTAN
BIKANER
JAISALMER
JODHPUR
JAIPUR
AJMER
BUNDI
GWALIOR

1

The Grand Trunk Road is a broad scratch across the shoulders of India and Pakistan, with Peshawar by the Khyber Pass in the North West Frontier Province of Pakistan at one end, and Howrah, on the Hooghly river opposite Calcutta, in India at the other. For nearly half its length it traverses what was once the undivided Punjab, the Land of the Five Rivers, the world of Kipling's *Kim*.

Colonization in India came from the north and spread to the Ganges Basin. Communication between the first important towns laid the foundation of the Northern Trunk route, developed in the fourth century BC by the Mauryans. This was still only a track centuries later, however, when Sher Shah Suri had a road laid out from Peshawar to Calcutta, with stone towers at intervals as milestones and serais for travellers to stay at overnight. This new road followed the alignment of the old track for much of the way.

Amenities for travellers along what came to be known as the Grand Trunk Road were added by succeeding Moghul monarchs, who built many more serais and had wells dug by the wayside. Prior to the middle of the nineteenth century, however, the road was impassable at most points for any sort of vehicular traffic.

Then the British built the present road, along the alignment of Sher Shah Suri's road in great part, metalling the surface and bridging all but a few of the many rivers, streams and gullies along the route.

The strategic value of the Grand Trunk Road was proved very soon after it had been built by the British, at the time of the Mutiny in 1857, when rapid large-scale movements across India were possible for the first time. Later many a recruit to the British army in India, including my grandfather, had his initiation into army life marching along the Grand Trunk Road. More recently the great road was a major supply route for both armies in the 1971 India-Pakistan struggle.

My own connection with the two countries traversed by the Grand Trunk Road has been a close one. I was born in India, in the foothills of the Himalayas, and lived there for fifteen years, until my family finally left India in 1950. My father taught at what was originally the Lawrence Royal Military School, and is now known as the Lawrence School, at Sanawar, near Kasauli, about forty-five miles by road from Simla, the old hill capital of India. My grandfather, who had been in the army, was later with the Church Missionary Society in Lahore, which is now in Pakistan, and although my sister and I spent by far the greater part of our time in the hills, we occasionally stayed for part of the long winter holidays with my grandparents in Lahore.

When I first had the opportunity to revisit India, and the Simla Hills in particular, I remembered various dicta on the folly of going back—but life has altered little in the hills. I was soon at home, and felt no more a stranger when travelling in India and Pakistan than, I imagine, would the citizens of these countries.

What I next wanted to do was to travel through both countries in a leisurely way, seeing some of their major cities but also seeing the country, for Pakistan and India are basically nations of smallholders. The prospect was so fascinating that it did not seem to need a justification. However, I needed a route, and on re-reading *Kim,* decided that the Grand Trunk Road, that mighty way 'bearing without crowding India's traffic for 1,500 miles—such a river of life as nowhere else exists in the world', would be the perfect route, and from recent visits I was convinced that life along its great length would, in many ways, have changed little since the days of Kim.

The journey was started in late January 1970—after a flight from England had brought me, within a day, from London mist to the glorious winter of the Punjab—and ended nearly four months later, in mid-May.

This book is the outcome. In it I may give the impression of being a linguist, and of understanding several dialects, but what I spoke during this journey was an amalgam of speeches, part remembered from my earliest years, when, so I have been told, I spoke my ayah's hill dialect, part the Hindustani picked up when I was older. This stew of speeches, which generous folk in North-West Pakistan called Urdu, genial Punjabis termed Punjabi, and the folk of the plains allowed was Hindustani, was enough for me to get by in basic matters, and when I met Pakistanis or Indians who were eager to discuss complex matters, it generally happened that they could speak

English. In the matter of foreign languages I am fortunate in being assisted by a lack of inhibition about grammar: if converse I must, then converse I do, 'with much noise and vociferation', as George Borrow recommended, and generally I find that I am understood.

My journey really began in Lahore, the heart of *Kim* country, where I caught a train for Peshawar, the start of the Grand Trunk Road. And what more suitable place could there be for starting a train journey than that self-same 'fort-like railway station' at which Kim and the Lama boarded the train for Ambala at the start of their joint adventures?

The name of my train too was just right—the *Khyber Mail.* The *Khyber Mail* had left Karachi the previous evening and was due into Lahore at 8 pm, by which time the third class carriages would certainly be very dirty, so I would need a seat. I therefore engaged a tall, broad-shouldered coolie, clad in the red shirt and pyjamas that are standard wear for coolies in Pakistan and India, and then relaxed, confident that he would give a doughty performance and get me a seat. While I waited, I bought a large, flaky, greasy paratha (a sort of thick chuppatti cooked in oil) from a railway platform stall, a paratha which was to colour my impressions over the next thirty-six hours. I ate what I could of it and then tried to rid myself of the remainder, first leaving it discreetly wrapped in newspaper in a corner—there being no dustbin in sight—and then, when a solicitous bystander returned it to me, leaving it at the end of a counter where a number of other articles were stacked, only to have it returned to me once again. Finally I rid myself of it during the rush to board the train.

When the train arrived, my coolie strode sturdily with my rucksack to a third class compartment door, but he could not prise it open because it was closed by the press of bodies from inside. He now stood stolidly under a window of the same compartment and it was clear that he was not prepared to do as the coolies of Old Delhi so often do, climb through the window. He thought though that I could manage, and indicated that I should climb on his knee and dive in from there. When I hesitated, he shouted that I would not travel far by standing still on the platform.

A moment later I had wriggled in at the window, pushed from behind by the coolie and pulled by a sporting passenger inside, and found myself on my back, lying on top of the other passengers who had just boarded and were struggling among the feet of those occupying the seats. Behind me another passenger was struggling to enter through the window and when he too had been hauled in, the passengers near the window shut it, the compartment by any standards now being full. This was a good idea, but unfortunately my rucksack was still outside, and no-one was heeding my coolie as he banged at the window. In the hubbub it was difficult to attract attention, but the window was opened at last and my rucksack pulled in. The window was promptly closed again, which left the coolie bellowing 'Paise, paise' on the other side, until after further pleas from myself the window was opened once again and the money passed out. I now tried to do what all those who had boarded at Lahore were trying to do, to create space, and eased myself into the knobbly gap between a tin trunk and a gunny-sack full of metal fittings, and was then able to look around.

All about me were big-boned, hard-muscled, fit-looking Pathans, men of the North West Frontier and its environs, members of a race whose activities had occupied the attention of the cream of British soldiery for nearly a century. They still looked wild, these men, though their border territory was now administered not by soldiers but by the Pakistani bureaucracy, and the border was no longer held by force but by printed agreements tabled with the United Nations. The days of the watchers on the hills with their rifles had gone, and the tribesmen whose clans were hereditary enemies were uniting to work at the hydro-electric and irrigation projects being built in their territories. Many of the men on the train were returning home after working in service or in factories at Karachi and Lahore, though it was difficult to imagine those tough highlanders submitting to industrial routine.

The compartment was similar to those of the same class on Indian trains, with a door at each end, and a gangway down the compartment running between single seats set back to back on one side, and two-tiered unpadded berths facing each other within small compartments open to the gangway, on the other. The bottom berths were divided into seat widths; the top berths were intended for baggage, but as was common practice, they were occupied by passengers. The top berths were the most coveted positions in a compartment, because by a tacit agreement, which applied throughout the sub-continent, if a man succeeded in spreading his bedroll on an unoccupied upper berth, he had staked a claim to it for his own use for as far as he was journeying. Thus the men on the top berths (fifteen inches wide and slightly tilted) were stretched out comfortably, while many of their fellow passengers were balanced in positions which no carriage designer could have conceived to be possible, some sitting on the back of single chairs, their feet braced against the partition wall across the gangway, others straddled across the gangway, with one foot on an armrest and the other on baggage or a clothes hook.

Most passengers, however, sat or lay either on baggage or directly on the floor, the density being greatest near the doors, the most convenient spot for people without tickets. Unfortunately the toilets too were situated near the doors, and these were therefore virtually inaccessible. This was not a great problem on Pakistani trains where women were strictly segregated and presumably travelled in less congested conditions, and men did not expect any concessions to comfort, but on Indian trains it could be an amusing experience watching a woman being passed from box to knee to head to shoulder, on her way to the toilet, and this would be especially entertaining if she were fat.

As a tightly-packed rucksack shakes down after a while, so our positions on the floor became more tenable after we had travelled some miles from Lahore on our way northwards. Had I been required to vote on the most uncomfortable passenger in the compartment, I would have chosen the middle-aged man perched on about one square foot of the luggage berth above me with his knees drawn up to his chin. I wondered how he managed to stay up there. I soon found out because he alighted at Gujranwala, the first station along the line, and the hospitable Pathans insisted that I have his vacant spot, not realizing that I could not accomplish his deep squat. I did manage to stay on my perch but I could not sleep lest I fell off. I doubt whether those on the floor slept either, though they closed their eyes between stations. Wazirabad Junction, Gujrat, Jhelum, Rawalpindi, Cambellpur, Nowshera Junction; the stations were happy respites in the long night when glasses of tea, musty cakes, and cigarettes were passed in through the windows. For some reason the collection of money was always left to the last moment by the vendors, and at every station there would be a commotion at departure as tea boys shouted for their money from the platform, and passengers shouted for their change.

Many of the Pathans alighted at Nowshera, the railhead for Swat, and I was then able to dismount from my perch, and stretch. An hour and a half later the *Khyber Mail* steamed into Peshawar Cantonment. It was 7 am and very cool.

The paratha I had eaten at Lahore Station had begun to exert its baleful influence on my stomach while I was still on the train, and by the time I alighted at Peshawar I was in a flaccid condition, and feeling so weak that I had difficulty in walking even without my rucksack. Enthusiasm had deserted me for the moment, but even so I was struck by the fertility of the cantonment area, where each bungalow had its neat garden and obvious promise of banks of flowers and cataracts of bougainvillaea on every garden wall later in the Spring. I was surprised by this aspect of what I had imagined as a harsh, dour, suspicious city, heavily fortified, lying in a dusty valley, overlooked by the lower ranges of the mountains that frame the frontier. I was to find that the old city did conform in some ways to what I had imagined; but the cantonment area was a huge garden culminating in the carefully tended acres of the campus of Islamia University where I found a bed at the Peshawar Youth Hostel, and stretched out gratefully for the rest of the morning. In the afternoon I went to a chemist to get some remedy for my disordered stomach, and he prescribed calcium bicarbonate tablets. He was offhand about the quantity I should take, suggesting 'five or six', but they were large tablets, and thinking that he had probably prescribed a Pathan-sized dose, I compromised and took three, and began to recover almost immediately.

The famous, old city of Peshawar was interesting more on account of the people who strode through its narrow streets than for the bazaars and architecture. The common dress of Pathan males was a loose grey shirt, baggy grey pantaloons and stout black sandals, a practical garb, which despite its lack of colour had considerable grace, and set off the feline strength of the big tribesmen. Afghans from across the border were more colourfully dressed, with embroidered waistcoats and tall turban cloths tied round golden head cones. Many of the men carried rifles or revolvers, and wore heavily laden bandoliers: the tradition of carrying arms had not yet died near the frontier.

The Peshawar bazaars had once been a major entrepôt for goods from Kabul and Bokhara. From Kabul had come raw silk, worsteds, cochineal, jalap, assafoetida, saffron, resin, and fruits both fresh and dried, and these goods had been exported from Peshawar to the

Punjab and other parts of the subcontinent. In exchange, English piece-goods, cambrics, silks, indigo, sugar and spices had been exported to Kabul. From Bokhara had come sequins and lace, and gold and silver thread, most of which had been exported to Kashmir whence the return trade was principally in shawls. With the advent of the railways, and the building of the Grand Trunk Road, Peshawar's importance as an entrepôt had declined. Among all the items I saw in the bazaars I was most impressed by the colour and delicacy of the china in use in every 'chaikhanna' (teahouse) I passed, where the big raw-boned customers drank from fine china cups, and the shelves above the earthenware ovens were lined with dainty little teapots decorated with pretty flower patterns. This chinaware was imported from China and Japan, but I also saw beautiful china made at a factory near Gujrat in Pakistan, where technical assistance was being given by Japanese advisers.

Fine dinner and tea services were not a modern innovation, however, for Peshawar had been noted for its glazed pottery in the days when the British first occupied the city in the middle of the nineteenth century, and traditional pottery of this kind, of a curious mixture of colours with green predominating, was still used for articles like storage jars and hookah bowls.

In the poorer chaikhannas, the little teapots and cups and saucers showed signs of frequent repairs. I saw a china-mender at work. He sat in the dust by the road clasping a cup between his feet, and drilled holes on either side of a crack with a diamond drill operated by a bow and string. He then set a brass clip into the holes and cemented it with a gum in which the white of eggs was the main ingredient. It was the work of a moment, and done so skilfully that the same piece could be repaired in many different places without a leak occurring anywhere.

Towards the end of my second day in Peshawar I had a down-at-heel shoe repaired. It was a fine evening; the sun was low over the hills of the frontier, the air was sweet and clean and I had a feeling of great well-being as I squatted on the hard earth near an entrance to the Islamia University where a grizzled old Pathan cobbler sat with a tall green hedge at his back, his last stuck into the earth before him, and offcuts of leather, mere scraps most of them, sorted into neat heaps according to thickness and size beside him. A few yards away squatted the guard at the gate, another old man, supporting a rifle between his knees.

The cobbler started on my shoes with a pair of pincers, working very deliberately and talking the while in soft tones to the guard. When the twisted nails were removed he started building up the heel with his repair scraps, using five or six pieces before the heel was level, and then he drew a greaseproof envelope from inside his grey shirt, shook out the little 'Blakey' (metal heel-plate) which was in it and showed it to me in the palm of his hand, as though it was a gem. Then before I could stop him he fixed it to the end of the already even heel like a monument, instead of setting it in flush with the leather. The guard looked at his friend's work wonderingly, and smiled with pride. The cobbler handed me the shoe and sat silent, looking at the ground; I think the very hills would have exclaimed in protest had I asked him to reset the 'Blakey'. He asked just six annas for his half-hour's work on the heel and that included the 'Blakey'.

I had no other repairs to be done and no provisioning was necessary, so I was ready for the Grand Trunk Road. I planned to start out next morning, and had the happy knowledge that the weather would almost certainly remain fine.

1 Before Rawalpindi—the camel is still a regular means of transport

2 Chaikhanna (teahouse) by the Grand Trunk Road at Hasan Abdal

3 Painted truck door

2

The first part of my journey would be through the North West Frontier Province, a province famous in the lore of British days because it was here, more than in any other part of the old undivided India, that military action could usually be guaranteed. Much of the province consists of mountainous ground, unfit for cultivation, and is the home of tough tribal people whose ancient customs of raiding the plains had provided plenty of activity for the British army. The Grand Trunk Road, however, passes through relatively fertile country, the Peshawar Valley itself being well irrigated and fertile.

The Indus marks the eastern boundary of the North West Frontier Province and beyond that I would enter the Punjab. Pakistan has a Punjab province and so does India: they are the major grain producing areas of their respective countries, and their peoples have for years been a major source of good soldiers for the armies of the subcontinent.

Before Independence and Partition in 1947, the two Punjabs had been united, but the border between India and Pakistan was drawn right through the Punjab and as a consequence the province suffered more than any other in either country at the time.

The people of this region are, however, famous for a resilience that has been built up over hundreds of years of invasions from the north-west, and today the areas of the Punjab on both sides of the border are again wealthy.

The Punjab means 'Five Rivers', and is a flat region through which flow five of the major rivers of the subcontinent—the Jhelum, Chenab, Ravi, Beas and Sutlej.

'A fair land,' said Kim, speaking of undivided India, 'a most beautiful land is this of Hind—and the land of the Five Rivers is fairer than all.'

I had much to look forward to.

As I had expected, the sun shone from a cloudless sky though the day was still a trifle chill, as I started off next morning on the first miles of the Grand Trunk Road.

The great road starts in front of Peshawar Cantonment station, passes the museum, skirts the formidable pile of Bala Hissar Fort, and comes to the outskirts of the city, from where it stretches straight ahead until it disappears in a haze on its way to Howrah near India's eastern border, nearly fifteen hundred miles away. A few tongas (horse-drawn carriages) were waiting to take passengers to outlying villages, and when I had passed these I was on my own.

Sometimes I do not fall into my stride for miles, but on this day I soon developed a rhythm, my feet sinking into the dusty strip on the edge of the road and raising little clouds at each step, my ruck-sack sitting comfortably on my shoulders. This was the pace to travel at, walking, or whenever I had the chance, riding on a bullock-cart, for this was a pace at which one could identify oneself with the countryside one passed through. At some stage of each day I would have to travel by bus or truck, or other such transport if I was to spend any time in the towns or cities en route, so I had resolved to accept a lift if I was offered one and to travel by local bus services when necessary, but to travel at walking pace for long periods each day, especially in the mornings. My first lift was not by bullock-cart, nor by truck, but on a mechanical monster, high up on the seat of an International Harvester bulldozer being carried on an articulated lorry. It shivered and rattled, and did not seem to be secured in any way, but it carried me safely for the six and a half miles it was going, and provided one of the most spectacular lifts I have had. Trees now lined the road and I could walk beside the fields in their shade, watching farmers scything the first of the wheat crop, and buffaloes padding their patient circles round water wheels. I became aware of the companionable silence of open, cultivated land, which is really a soft sound of hidden things, and this though I was on the Grand Trunk Road, the greatest road in the subcontinent; the road had been there too long to mar the spirit of the countryside and the sound of an occasional truck travelling on it was absorbed by the warm still earth.

Pathan hospitality and courtesy are legendary, and I experienced it when I accepted the offer of a short lift in a small cart pulled by a single bullock, driven by an old man in a white skull cap, white shirt and white pyjamas. He wasn't going far, only two miles, but as he was about to turn off down a track lined with orange trees he invited me to have tea, and I continued with him to a walled enclosure set two hundred yards back from the road. We stopped by a small opening in the side of the mud wall at which he dismounted and entered, and a moment later I was greeted with open arms by a brisk, grey-bearded man who welcomed me as though I was a favourite son. I had come to the household of a local landowner, a Khan, and, having delivered me, the old man who had brought me there went off to the fields in his cart.

My host, a short, very stocky Pathan in his fifties, hurried me into the unpaved courtyard within the walls, barking orders to people out of sight and growling that I must be worn out in this heat with such a load. Against the inner wall was a small reed shelter containing a charpai (string bed), a table and a chair, and when I was comfortably settled on the charpai, the Khan reminisced about British friends with whom he had hunted before the war, one Mr Holdsworth in particular who had at that time been Principal of Islamia College, Peshawar, and a great friend of his father's. To Mr Holdsworth he gave the accolade by saying: 'He was a very brave man, a very fine shot and a real Pathan.' Weeks later I learned that this old friend of the Khan's was R. L. Holdsworth who had climbed Kamet on F. S. Smythe's Expedition, and had acquired greater fame by smoking his pipe on the summit. Shooting was the Khan's great passion, and he promised to show me his guns: but first he insisted that I must eat. My conventionally deprecating reply drew the rejoinder: 'A true traveller should eat whenever food is set before him.' I set to on a plate of parathas and followed this by drinking about two pints of tea. The Khan was now satisfied, and declared: 'You are our guest; you have eaten with us; you are always our friend.' His rifles were now brought out, all three of First World War vintage, all in excellent condition. He agreed that a rifle was not as necessary now as it had been before the Second World War, but even now, he asserted, he could shoot the sharp edge of a knife blade from across the compound. 'If a thief came to our home at night and made the slightest sound . . . ptt! . . . he would be dead.' I had no doubt whatever that what he said was true, and other men who had joined us looked on with great respect. It was evident that to be a good shot in these parts was still as desirable an accomplishment as to be a good swordsman in seventeenth-century Europe. One of his rifles was a British Army .303 presented to him with a citation for bravery as a reward for catching a notorious dacoit (bandit). Another was a 7 mm Westley Richards which he had had with him in 1948, when the tribesmen of the North West Frontier region marched upon Kashmir, and Indian troops were flown in just in time to halt them on the outskirts of Srinagar. He slapped the butt of the rifle as he recalled how he had shot down an Indian plane with this rifle by killing the pilot. Nowadays, he complained, shooting was an expensive hobby, with 7 mm rounds selling at 2 rupees 4 annas each.

He pressed me to stay for the night, but I declined because I had just started my journey and had come too short a way. So I set off again, after an escort of four men, each armed with a rifle, had brought me the two hundred yards to the road.

It was now past midday and all traffic appeared to have stopped except for a string of buffaloes and bullocks going towards Peshawar, and for some miles I saw no-one afoot. After I had passed through the township of Pabbi and was in the open country beyond, it seemed that even Nature was slumbering. The Grand Trunk Road stretched straight ahead, deserted, and walking seemed pointless just then because I too was beginning to feel drowsy after all the parathas I had eaten. I had enjoyed my bullock-cart ride that morning and hoped that another cart would appear from a side road; it had only been a small cart, built by the local 'mistry' (carpenter) at a cost of 400 rupees but it had groaned and jolted ponderously just like large carts double its size which were normally drawn by two bullocks, and riding on it I had felt that rather exciting affinity with the timbers in their motion that one feels on a wooden ship in a stiff wind, when one does not merely ride in, but becomes a part of, the vessel.

No bullock-cart appeared, and I was glad to accept a lift in a truck, and came into Nowshera sitting atop a high load of corrugated iron. Nowshera was a quiet cantonment town near the Kabul river, which flows from Afghanistan and converges with the Indus twenty miles south eastward at Attock. I was accosted by two men near the bus station, wild looking characters with scarred faces and furtive expressions who assured me against all probability that they only wished to assist me 'because you are a stranger'. I reluctantly accepted an invitation to a cup of tea in the bus-station tea room, a fly sanctuary, and learned that my acquaintances' homes were in Dir, a state in Pakistan to the north of Peshawar, on the border with Afghanistan, which until recently had rarely been visited by foreigners and had been run with little interference from the central government by a ruler of feudal mould. I was interested to learn that they considered themselves to be Afghans.

'The tribal peoples and Afghans on the border are all the same', one explained, and asked me what I thought of Pakistan. Having entered the country via Lahore, I was accustomed to meeting fervent Nationalists, so now I made my usual laudatory reply, but this elicited no pleasure from my acquaintances.

'Pah!' retorted the one who had questioned me, 'this country is small and powerless. Peshawar, Lahore, Rawalpindi, Karachi, buss! that is all. But in British days to Calcutta, and Bombay: that was an Empire!' It appeared that they were in sympathy with those demanding an independent border territory.

After leaving the two men from Dir I took the wrong turning for the Grand Trunk Road, and though the way was nearly deserted those I met assured me that I was on the right road, so I kept on walking until a car stopped beside me and the driver, pointing to a small cairn about ten yards ahead, told me: 'If you go beyond the stones there, you will be in tribal area and in trouble.' Tribal independence it appeared had not quite died when the British departed. Fifteen minutes later, on the Grand Trunk Road, I encountered an officious little man who presented some kind of identity card and demanded to see my passport. As this had somehow sunk to the bottom of my pack I was rather irritated by the time I was free to start again, and to ensure that I wasted no more time in this military township I decided to hitch-hike. Pakistan must be one of the best countries in the world to hitch-hike in, for it happened now, and it was to happen again, that I had no sooner attracted a truck-driver's attention than he stopped for me; such ease does rob hitch-hiking of the pleasure one feels at getting a lift when conditions are difficult—but I have never heard a hitch-hiker complain that lifts came too easily.

The truck was a Bedford, but apart from the name on the bonnet it was difficult to recognize it as such, because nearly every square inch of woodwork on the high tray and the platform above the cab was painted with idealized representations of gardens and mountains, birds and flowers and trees; more practically, the contractor's telephone number was displayed on a panel beneath an illustration of a slender milky hand reaching for a telephone. The truck looked more like a mobile Art Gallery, or a medieval pageant, than the modern vehicle it was. The interior of the cab had not been neglected and everything had been done to ensure that art and comfort should not be sacrificed to viewing space. All sharp edges in the cab were covered with thick padded plastic material that encroached on window space, and the area of free windscreen was further reduced by garlands of flowers suspended from the roof, and by little bags containing lucky charms given to the driver by his father, which also hung in front of the windscreen. The small side windows had been filled in with mirror glass leaving only little heart-shaped spaces free. Nearly all the trucks I had seen in this region were painted like this, and many a man earned a living as a truck artist. Though truck decoration is a recognized art throughout the subcontinent I had never before seen such elaborate artwork as that on Pathan trucks, and I was to find as I continued along the Grand Trunk Road that trucks were less colourful the further east I went.

The driver of the truck was the owner, and he also owned a second truck which was being driven by his brother. The trucks were the fruit of six years' work as a concreting supervisor on the Warsak Dam site eighteen miles north west of Peshawar, a project that had provided work lucrative enough to draw tribes which had been hereditary enemies for centuries to work together. The driver had done well, and now had a contract to cart stones needed for road-works. The source of the stones was forty miles from the repair site, and he received two hundred rupees for every load carried. Later I was to meet a small camel train, carrying bricks along an eleven-mile stretch between Gujrat and Lalamusa on the Grand Trunk Road. Each camel could carry a load of 640 lbs three times a week between the two places, and each was attended by a man who received ten rupees per trip. When I came upon the camels they were unladen and the men could, if they wished, ride, but in fact they walked most of the way; when the camels were laden the men just walked. I did not discover the relative costings for operating the truck and the camels, but it was easy to see that the truck owner was the prince of the road.

When I boarded the truck it was not carrying its usual load of stones but baled tobacco, and I sat on top of the bales, level with the roof of the cab. We passed through harsh, hilly country and the road narrowed as we skirted the hills above the Kabul River, passing a long string of unladen camels on the way. Then the broad bed of the Indus became visible, and we could see Attock Fort guarding the confluence of the two rivers. It was just when I sighted the fort that a sudden gust of wind blew my straw hat off, blew it over the edge of the road, and I saw it sailing into space above the river. I hope it floated long enough on the Kabul to reach the Indus, the main river of the Punjab; it was a strange end for a hat bought in a smart shop in Colabar, Bombay. After that mishap I wore make-shift headgear, a handkerchief with knots tied at its four corners.

We crossed the Indus on a combined rail and road bridge, five hundred yards long and built between 1880 and 1883 to replace a boat bridge further upstream. A large sign indicated that we had entered the Punjab and the driver celebrated by buying garlands of marigolds to hang from the windscreen. Another large notice stated that this was 'Prohibited Territory', which meant that photography was proscribed, the authorities in Pakistan being extremely sensitive about bridges and forts, whether they were of legitimate tourist interest or not. The fort had been built in Akbar's reign at which time the Indus had been crossed by a ferry operated by boatmen from a little village near the foot of the hill on which the fort stands. It had been a dangerous crossing for the small vessels, and Akbar had settled land on the intrepid boatmen, whose descendants still live in the village.

Attock was my destination for the night and I had intended to stay at the PWD Inspection bungalow on a hillock within sight of the fort but the sulky chowkidar (a watchman, in charge of the property) turned me away, saying that the bungalow was booked for the night, and that he could only give me a bed if I had a pass. My argument that it was unlikely all those who had passes for the night would actually arrive, was unavailing, and I had no help from any of the guests already there; one of them was so demoralized by the place that he laughed when I was turned away. Attock also had a Civil Resthouse, but here too I was told that all the rooms were booked for the Deputy Commissioner and his party, who were to attend the opening of a terrace garden near the banks of the Indus next day. In that case, I said, I proposed to sleep on the verandah, but this chowkidar was no more forthcoming than his counterpart at the PWD bungalow, until a Pathan, the District Engineer's driver, persuaded him to give me a room on the understanding that I would vacate it if the official party arrived. The matter of passes at these official resthouses and bungalows was a vexing one; in many instances they were fully booked and there was no other accommodation available, but because payment was not asked in advance and there was no penalty for failing to use booked accommodation, the booking system was misused; duplicate reservations were made by travelling officials weeks before a tour against the possibility, not the certainty or even probability, that accommodation might be needed.

The view from the Civil Resthouse must have been magnificent after the rains when the Kabul and Indus were in spate, but now the river beds were broad expanses of sand broken by narrow channels of water. Nevertheless the scene possessed some grandeur, with harsh brown hills in the foreground framing the fan-shaped valley of the meeting river beds, and misty blue mountains to the north in the background. One day perhaps a hotel would stand nearby, with rooms overlooking the river, but I was seeing what the earliest travellers to this spot would have seen except for the road skirting the shore below the resthouse, which had been built only 120 years before I arrived.

The hillocks between the resthouse and the fort were dotted with ruins, some of them like small watch-towers, others remnants of some old wall, but one ruin was still in fair condition and was especially interesting because it had been a serai, the first of the great Moghul serais I had encountered along the Grand Trunk Road. This was the Begum-ki-Serai, built in the reign of the Emperor Jehangir. It had walls four feet thick in most places, broad ramparts, sunken cubicles for men and horses, and a broad courtyard with a small mosque at the centre. It was pleasant to speculate on the rough company of caravaneers who had once gathered there after the dangerous crossing of the river, and on the soldiers who had guarded the place. Now, however, the courtyard was a sportsfield for troops from the fort, who were playing rounders when I arrived, and the officer who was umpiring the game warned me gravely not to take photographs. The people of the Punjab are as a rule quick to smile but like everyone else I met in Attock the soldiers eyed me unsmilingly. I found that I could still manage a grin, but felt that if I remained in Attock much longer I too would lose the faculty of being able to do so.

What was wrong with Attock? Perhaps the snakes were to blame. I had not seen any, but the following is an extract from Murray's *Handbook of the Punjab* for 1883, when the serai was being used as an officers' mess:

'Close to the Mess is a place where the Commandant was attacked by a serpent which pursued him and almost overtook him in a narrow path, with a precipice of twenty feet on one side and a perpendicular rock on the other, and he had to drop down from that height to escape. He was not hurt and obtained a lantern and club and killed the snake. The fact is, the fort and its vicinity swarm with snakes and scorpions. The same night the sentry was attacked by a serpent which he killed with his bayonet. These reptiles render Atak, which would otherwise be a pleasant station, disagreeable and dangerous.'

Or perhaps the local inhabitants were to blame. They had some strange customs and superstitions in the days when Hindus as well as Moslems lived in Attock, and it was likely that the superstitions were retained after Independence. One of the ways by which locals had tried to induce rain after the summer was by surrounding a particularly holy man or perhaps some visiting official and dousing him with water until he prayed for rain; this was reckoned to be very effective. Even more powerful than this, the locals believed, was the old scolds method, whereby the inhabitants of Attock assembled together and gathered pots full of water and dung and compost of various kinds, which they took to the house of the person rated to be the most quarrelsome resident in the village. The victim must have known what was about to happen when he saw his fellow villagers advancing on his home with their malodorous loads and much of the fun must have been derived from listening to his expostulations and threats. After a pause, perhaps in order to let the victim become thoroughly roused, the pots and their contents would be thrown into his house, and it was the ensuing violent argument that was supposed to attract the attention of the Almighty, and apprise Him of the desperate need of the village for the rains.

As I had expected, not one of the officials who had reserved beds at the Civil Resthouse for the night arrived, and I became the only guest, or the only one who signed the visitors' book, I should say, because a number of the chowkidar's friends occupied the main suite in the bungalow and caused me some uneasy moments until I fell asleep, as the door between their room and mine could not be bolted from my side.

The morning brought a pleasant surprise when I left the arid hump of Attock, and came almost immediately into fertile open country with the Grand Trunk Road running straight again, between fields of vegetables. The road was bordered by tali trees but even without their shade it was cool at that early hour and the colours around me were gentler than they would appear later in the day. The brightest objects were two white-breasted kingfishers, which were either very nervous of me or very curious, because they flew from tree to tree ahead of me as I walked along. It was very quiet and the only sound was the groan of the occasional Persian water wheel, and the chattering of parrots. This was a relatively underpopulated part of the Punjab, and I anticipated more activity further south, though nothing like the 'river of life' carried by the Grand Trunk Road in Kim's days.

The first vehicle to appear, a jeep, stopped for me, and I came just before midday to the town of Hasan Abdal, thirty-one miles from Attock.

Here by the Grand Trunk Road I found a teahouse that would have been recognized by travellers of centuries ago, set in the open, with three charpais ranged beneath a small cluster of shisham trees. The proprietor dispensed tea from behind the traditional clay oven, and chatted with his customers. It was the best of places from which to watch the world go by.

In Hasan Abdal stands the important Sikh shrine of Panja Sahib, which, according to legend, marks the spot where Guru Nanak, the founder of Sikhism, once came, tired and expecting the hospitality of a local Moslem saint, Baba Wali Kandahari. As legend has it, however, he received scant courtesy, because Baba Wali was affronted by what he considered to be the Guru's presumption, and threw a boulder at him, which was several tons in weight. Guru Nanak caught the great rock and in doing so left the imprint of his fingers on it. He then commanded water to flow from the boulder and it did. It is this same stone, the Sikhs believe, which is kept in a tank by the temple, and which is said to be the source of a spring that keeps the tank full.

When India was partitioned in 1947, the Sikhs left what had become West Pakistan, and so the Panja Sahib temple is empty for most of the year, but at Baisakhi, the spring festival, a traditional time for Sikhs to make a pilgrimage to their major shrines, hundreds of Sikhs come to Hasan Abdal from India.

At that time the locals make a rival pilgrimage to the shrine of Baba Wali, he who had cast the boulder at the Guru, at the summit of a hill on the east of the town. The way to this shrine is rather steep, but the view from the top makes the climb worthwhile, for one can see far over the surrounding plain. Nine miles east lies Taxila, where ruined cities are still being excavated, and beyond lies the Margala Pass, dominated by the tall memorial column to John Nicholson. Many an invading army has crossed this plain, but the sound of their tread must have been muffled by the sheer size of this landscape.

I was just beginning to be affected by the afternoon heat, and was soon drenched with perspiration when I started off again with my rucksack on the Grand Trunk Road. However, this was a very hospitable road, and once again I was given a lift, one remarkable for the reaction of the driver and his mate to a girl being given a ride on the carrier of a young man's bicycle. As we neared this pair it was impossible to see anything of the girl under her black burqa except a pair of black shoes—a depressingly modest sight, but both the Pathans in the truck whistled and hooted as we passed, explaining to me that she was a prostitute, a 'jig-a-jig girl'. I concluded that they knew the girl. They were still discussing her when I alighted at Serai Kala, the turning for Taxila, which was two and a half miles away. A tonga-wallah (the wallah is the man in charge) promptly asked five times the correct fare to take me to Taxila and I wondered that anyone could still believe I had money enough to comply with such requests: it was obvious that other travellers with rucksacks had paid without first bargaining.

My accommodation that night was to be Taxila youth hostel, and I was pleased to find that this was a modern building. However, it was in the charge of a very odd warden indeed, who looked rather like an illustration of Rumpelstiltskin, small, bald-headed, with a red-dyed beard, and a malevolent expression on his face. His teeth were broken and discoloured, his voice was harsh, and he spoke very fast in a mixture of Urdu and Pushtu which was very nearly unintelligible. He looked at me suspiciously as I strode cheerfully in at the front door, his left eye blue, distrustful and half closed, his right eye brown and staring fixedly with no more animation than a marble. He seemed to be as nervous and excitable as Ben Gunn—I would not have been at all surprised if he had asked whether I had any cheese in my rucksack—but he had none of the affability of that marooned seafarer. When I tendered money for the night he scrutinized each coin and rejected three before he was satisfied—apparently some of the coins in use in Lahore were not legal tender here in the north—and he was even dissatisfied with the colour of a rupee note.

'You'll be going tomorrow?' he suggested in a wheedling tone, and scowled when I refused to confirm this. It was certainly the oddest reception I had ever had at a youth hostel. Before he allocated me a room he handed me an enormous padlock, then showed me into my quarters on the side of the building, adjacent to his own. The most phlegmatic visitor would have been unnerved by his subsequent behaviour; first he asked me to bolt the door, then the windows, then to try the lock in the attached toilet and to make sure that the windows in there could be bolted. When he was satisfied that I could make everything fast he pulled the charpai, the only furniture in the room, into a corner and advised me to place my rucksack beneath the window so that it could not be seen by anyone peering in. I asked whether it would not have been simpler to provide curtains but he only muttered to himself and appeared not to understand me.

'Good, good,' he chuckled to himself, 'everything locked.' He then asked me to let him out through the entrance door, and to make it fast behind him, and I was then to let myself out from the rear. When I left for the bazaar he peered from his window and wanted to know whether I was absolutely sure that I had bolted my door.

Beyond the hostel was the Taxila Museum, and beyond that the excavations began, the ditches and mounds stretching for miles, all that remained of once great cities founded by the Greeks and the Kushan Kings. It was interesting to see the artefacts and sculptures in the Museum, brought not from thousands of miles away but from just beyond the Museum garden; for a moment it was easy to imagine that I was somewhere by the Mediterranean as I looked at the sculptures but then the prominent notice in the foyer caught my eye again, 'Guns, rifles, revolvers, sword sticks and umbrellas must be left with the Attendant', and I was once again in the harsh landscape of northern Pakistan.

A talkative doctor in the bazaar recommended a local eating-house. 'Where they have chuppattis,' he explained and then added jocularly, 'and it was by digesting such chuppattis that we were able to defeat India.' This was the first reference of this sort to India I had heard since my arrival in North West Pakistan; I was to find that the obsession over Kashmir, and the urge to prepare for war again was greater as I approached the Indian frontier. The belief that Pakistan had triumphed in the last conflict, in 1965, seemed to be well rooted in people's minds, and they had evidently been exposed to considerable propaganda on the radio and in the Press.

The eating-house which had been recommended had many praiseworthy features: it was little more than the usual bazaar stall, but the food was delicious and service was prompt, and the little waiter, a boy of about twelve, who carried chuppattis to diners in his hands, had no notion of getting a tip. Many customers were imperious and bellowed for service the moment that they required anything, wasting no time over their food. By contrast, two elderly men who had been shown into a little room at the rear, where the only furniture was a charpai, conversed over their food in a most courtly manner, and when they had eaten, and drunk tea, they remained sitting cross-legged on the charpai talking gravely and effortlessly, and it was clear that their talk followed some ritual pattern familiar and pleasant to them both; here was one small corner where people had retained the art of conversation.

The famous chuppattis recommended by the doctor were prepared at the front of the forecourt in a tandoor, a large earthenware pot set in a pit and surrounded by hot coals. This tandoor was about the size of the jars in which the forty thieves came to a painful end in the story of Ali Baba. One man made all the chuppattis for the diners, and this meant quite a number when each man could eat about ten. The dough was made from wholemeal flour and water and was beaten into little cakes in the hands, then flattened by hand, and patted onto the inside of the jar, each taking only a few seconds to prepare. The chuppatti cook worked with amazing speed, his brow and his lean uncovered torso gleaming with perspiration. When the chuppattis had been in the tandoor for half a minute or so, they were whisked out with a metal rod rather like a long poker with a bend at the tip, and served directly. It was clear from the speed at which the chuppatti maker worked that he belonged to no union.

Night came very suddenly, and the road was invisible as I returned towards the youth hostel, which was on the very outskirts of the small town and some hundred yards beyond the last dwelling. Thinking of the odd warden, I was feeling nervous, and when a car coming from behind me stopped, I not only refused a lift but eyed the driver with great suspicion. The old warden was waiting for me, peering out from his window.

'Hurry up, hurry up,' he rasped, 'it is late.' It was 7.30 pm.

'Are you going tomorrow?' he asked, but I didn't answer him. I could hear him shuffling about for a while in his room before he settled down for the night. In my own bare, curtainless room I felt in a state of siege as I sat on my charpai, reading. The night was very still, and the only sound was the old man's cough which rumbled as if we were in a tomb.

'You're going today?' he jabbered as soon as I appeared next morning. It was more a statement than a question. 'If you're not out by 10 am I get another eight annas from you.' He glared balefully at me, and seemed to be shaken with rage when I merely smiled. When he finally knew that I was leaving he mellowed and showed me where I could have a wash—there was no water from the taps in the hostel—and agreed to be photographed.

The Margala Pass is five dusty miles from Serai Kala and an appropriate setting for the great polygonal memorial to John Nicholson because the Margala hills form the eastern boundary of the land which Pathans consider their homeland, and Nicholson did much of his service in their country, so impressing the tribesmen that after his death a religious sect grew up which considered Nicholson its deity.

A stone slab inside the column bore the legend:

> 'This column is erected by friends, British and Native, to the Memory of Brigadier General John Nicholson CB who after taking a hero's part in four great wars for the defence of British India
>
> Cabul 1840
> 1st Sikh War 1845
> 2nd Sikh War 1848
> Sepoy Mutiny 1857
>
> and being as renowned for his civil rule in the Punjab as for his share in its conquest, fell mortally wounded on 14th September in leading to victory the main column of assault at the Great Siege of Delhi and died 23rd September 1857 aged 34. Mourned by the two races with an equal grief.'

The monument and its approaches were in very good condition and I was impressed to see a relic of British days so respectfully tended. Below the monument, three stone tablets had been set into the rocky wall of the cutting which was the pass, one a replica of that I had seen in the column, the second a translation from this into Urdu; and the third stated in English:

> 'Nicholson was killed at Delhi in 1857 by the Freedom Fighter Kale Khan.'

By the addition of a single plaque the honours of war had been shared.

The Pass lies sixteen miles from Rawalpindi. The capital was my destination for the night, and I felt that I could get there by nightfall after a leisurely walk. So I sat down on a dry-stone wall on the east of the Pass, and lit my pipe with a feeling of great well-being. The only habitation in sight was a mud-walled farmhouse set in fields of grain at the foot of the ridge on which the monument stood, and from the shoulder of the hill above the Pass I had seen an old man squatting in the courtyard smoking his hookah, oblivious of the watcher on the heights. This was an era of peace, but in former days the old man would not have sat so tranquilly there, out in the open and within easy range of a rifle bullet. Apart from this farmhouse I appeared to have all the land, for as far as I could see, to myself. My pipe was drawing well, I had an interesting destination for the evening, and my shoulders were free of my rucksack. This was one of those moments which leave a powerful memory to lure one out onto the road again.

Now something very unusual occurred. In Pakistan one does not expect to have many chances of seeing a young woman's face, and one certainly does not expect to be addressed by a young woman, but a small modern saloon car stopped beside me, and a strikingly attractive young woman who might have stepped straight from the *Arabian Nights* tales, wound down a window and addressed me in English. I felt then something of the awe with which some poor man in the days of Haroun al Raschid would have beheld that forbidden sight, the face of a princess.

She asked whether I was going to Rawalpindi, and whether I would accept a ride. Her own car was chauffeur-driven, and four women were in the rear seat, all eyeing me covertly and with some amusement. Their baggage car was following; I could ride in that. When this second car arrived I climbed into the vacant front seat, with the rucksack on my lap, and this so amused the two women sitting in the rear that they giggled all the way to Rawalpindi.

The young lady in the leading car was obviously someone of rank, because when I alighted at Rawalpindi a number of men hurried forward and shook me very respectfully by the hand. Those who had not seen my mode of arrival, however, judged correctly from my appearance that I was unlikely to boost the economy: it was a sad contrast.

Rawalpindi is a cantonment town that had a moment of glory before the new capital of Pakistan was built at Islamabad, and while it was the temporary capital the saloon cars of foreign diplomats had surged up and down the Mall, the gleaming dark Cadillacs moving nose to tail as their drivers passed the time along what must be the most elegant stretch of the Grand Trunk Road.

The elegant past still appeared to be reflected in Rawalpindi's price lists however, and I decided to press on, to find another halting place for the night.

Within moments of my reaching the outskirts of 'Pindi a truck drew up alongside, and I travelled the next twenty miles with a ferocious-looking Pathan who informed me with great vigour that the flag of Islam would one day 'fly throughout the whole world'.

Then followed another truck ride, and this time the driver and his mate were quite the wildest looking pair I had travelled with. Their truck was in very poor condition. Every few minutes a red light on the dashboard indicated that the engine was overheating. We would stop, the driver's mate would jump out and place stones under the front wheels, and we would wait for five minutes or so before starting off again. Progress was very slow, and as the sun neared the horizon I began to think that I might have to spend the night in the truck, an unwelcome prospect because I did not trust my companions.

We passed through wild broken country near the hills of the Salt Range, where the earth was a reddish colour, very dry and cast in fantastic shapes, rather like the broken country scarred with narrow gullies and outcrops of rock that is the background for many Western films.

The victims of recent accidents lay here and there along the way: a disembowelled donkey, its skin still partly intact; the skeleton of a camel; the spectacular wreck of a Burmah Shell tanker buried in the side of a gaily-painted truck, a sombre scene in the fading light.

At a very lonely point in the road we picked up a weird flapping figure, a man with long hair and a staff and a begging bowl. I could

4 Relaxing by the Grand Trunk Road, Pakistani style, near Jhelum

5 Roadside barber, Lahore

6 'Prime bananas, succulent grapes'— a roadside fruit-stall

not guess what he had been doing so far away from the nearest settlement, and the driver did not ask questions, just told him to jump on at the back. It was now that I began to think that I had done my new acquaintances an injustice, but had no chance to make amends for my churlishness, for they turned off the Grand Trunk Road twelve miles before Jhelum, a city on the west bank of the Jhelum river.

3

The sky above the burnt orange sunset was still steely blue when by luck I found a bus destined for Jhelum city. When I tendered my fare the conductor refused to accept it and the passengers around me nodded their approval of his action.

'You see, it is a tradition here in Pakistan that we do not like our guests to pay,' explained a man sitting near me. He seemed shy at first but was soon dilating on the greatness of Pakistan, of her success in the war against India, and of the perfidy of the Hindus who had 'stabbed the Moslems in the back'. When he had concluded his peroration I cleared my throat and he was instantly all courtly attention. I asked whether he could recommend an inn at Jhelum. He shook his head gloomily.

'Jhelum possesses no hotels suitable to your status,' he said with a charming deference which was all the more moving because there seemed so little cause for it. He named one hotel which he suggested was rather better than the others, but another passenger disagreed.

'Better he should go to the Karachi Hotel,' he advised, 'where they charge one rupee less and the bedclothes are clean.'

The promise of clean bedclothes was enough to lure me to the recommended hotel, a flat-roofed single-storey inn built round three sides of a mud square. The rooms were like cells, with red brick floors, plaster walls, and windows with shutters and bars, but all the necessary facilities were provided, a fan, a table, a naked electric light and, as I had been promised, a clean mattress and sheets, all for the charge of three rupees per night. The toilet facilities were adequate, two pumps and two open drain latrines, the pumps being sited next to and slightly uphill of the latrines so that a fairly constant flow of water kept the drains clean.

When I arrived the manager was sitting with friends and guests at a table under the outermost branches of a tall banyan tree in the centre of the courtyard. They must have been there since well before the sun set and were so engrossed in their conversation that they did not move the table into the light cast into the courtyard by a street lamp. Each man rose and introduced himself with grave courtesy, and they all expressed satisfaction at my decision to stay there the night.

Later, sitting in the courtyard, I heard singing and went to investigate. On the corner of the street was a small fruit and vegetable bazaar, and though traders were still doing business, most of them seemed to be clearing their shelves and preparing for the morrow. One fruitseller, however, seemed to have lost all interest in business. A dozen men were seated in front of his stall in the faint orange light of a hurricane lamp, and one of their number was the singer. He was completely absorbed in a song epic of the life of the Prophet Mohammed, and his audience, listening with closed eyes, shook their heads to the slow rhythm, crying 'Wah' whenever the Prophet was mentioned.

The fruitseller, a thin, dreamy-eyed old man with a silky white beard, sat on a platform surrounded by half-empty baskets containing oranges, guavas and a few discs of sliced sugar-cane on which flies were gathered like dry moss on a rock. The singer was a big man with strong, regular features, dressed in a shirt open to his waist, and a loin-cloth. He sang with such fervour that the veins in his neck jutted and pulsated; his fists were clenched, and even his calf muscles were so taut that periodically his legs trembled like those of a climber too long in one stance. When he had finished his song he slowly relaxed, and noticing me for the first time asked what I thought of his singing. Satisfied by my reply, he offered to sing again, better and longer. But first he would prepare his throat, and he did this by smoking a 'Scissors', one of the cheapest cigarettes available in the bazaar. And he ate pan (betel-leaf, wrapped round areca nut, lime and other ingredients, and chewed as a digestive).

One of the audience explained meanwhile that the singer had brought goods to the market that morning from a village thirty miles away—Jhelum is the headquarters and main market of the district—and that business concluded, he was in the mood to sing. The song was a traditional one: occasionally the singer extemporized, but everyone knew the words and could appreciate variations.

I was not surprised when the singer, having finished his cigarette, was wracked by a harsh cough, but he soon settled, gazed at the stars shining brightly in a cloudless sky, then started singing. He was oblivious of cars which hooted as they passed, of the clopping of horses' hooves, and of that most distracting of sounds, the admonition of the tonga-wallahs to their horses as they tried to make them trot, which was an alternate hissing and clucking.

Two stalls away a boy was on his knees pounding dough on a large circular metal plate, and the pit-a-pat sound he made was a counterpoint to the song. By the time I departed the singer had commenced yet another song, and it was clear that the fruitseller had forgotten about cleaning his stall.

The sky early next morning was a clear pale blue, and beggars were already at their stations under the railway bridge, raising stubs of hands for alms, as I continued on my way. These beggars sat on either side of the road, a couple of yards apart, and each man appeared to have created a neat cubicle for himself, an office in the open air. On the outskirts of Jhelum was a shop bearing the proud title 'Up-to-date and latest furniture' and then the Grand Trunk Road came to open country again. The road was embanked here and an enterprising young man was lying on a charpai wedged between the embankment and a shady tree. A quarter of a mile further on was the Jhelum, one of the great rivers of the Punjab, which rises in the mountains visible on the northern horizon, the Pir Pinjals. The river was low at this time, and from the mile-long bridge crossing it one looked down on broad islands of white sand divided by narrow channels of dirty brown water. I kept close to the rail on the bridge but even so cyclists seemed to steer directly at me; one rider thudded into my side and continued again without stopping, apparently without noticing that he had hit anything. Like London commuters these men were oblivious of everything but the need to keep moving. One fellow, however, called out: 'Have you not got plenty money of thee pocket?' and looked very indignant.

On the east bank of the river was an encampment of nomad herdsmen, living in rude tents surrounded by rush mat screens. Their buffaloes were grazing near the river and would soon be on their way to higher pastures in the hills. A man and a boy were making rush mats beside the road, deftly threading the rushes through taut strings an inch apart and twenty feet long, stretched from poles fastened to stakes in the ground. The pair worked so fast that their fingers seemed to pass in and out through the strings with the rushes.

Nearby was a small bazaar and a grain market. As I passed the bazaar a man ran after me shouting an invitation to me to drink tea, and in case I did not understand Urdu he grasped my arm and led me to his teahouse, where, exhorting his other customers to give me space, he set up a table and chair for me in the centre of the room. Having brought a large pot of tea he retired to his corner, watching attentively to see that I wanted for nothing, while his customers smoked their hookahs and gazed at me gravely without speaking. It was almost as if they were engaged in a sacred ritual, so deeply was the urge to give hospitality ingrained in their natures.

The neighbouring grain market was nearly empty, and most of the dealers sat reading in front of their cavernous stores. A few camels were being loaded by a well in the centre of the high-walled courtyard, but business would be slack until the harvest was brought in. The market was on the edge of a town named Serai Alamgir, which had been built, the locals informed me, round a fort and serai dating from Akbar's time. The place was much patronized by flies and was a disappointment because little remained of Moghul buildings except a small mosque.

Once more in rural Pakistan, I met old acquaintances, the truck-driver and his mate who had taken me to Attock. They were now carrying stones to a road-building site at Lalamusa, twenty miles on. Beyond that was a stretch of the Grand Trunk Road just like that described by the old Ressaldar to the Lama and Kim: a broad metalled middle road taking the fast traffic, and dusty unmetalled side-lanes for the slow traffic, the three ways being divided by shady trees. I kept to the shade of a side lane by the fields and was accosted at the first village I came to by one who said that his friend would like to converse with me: would I be so kind as to retrace my steps just a few yards? I expected to be presented to a dignified old man, but found instead a whale of a fellow lying on a charpai under a banyan tree, a fellow too idle to turn round and face me even when I was announced. I waited silently so that he had to turn round, and this he eventually did, regarding me with bright little eyes sunk deep in a pumpkin of a face . . . As he continued to regard me inscrutably, I prepared to leave, but his fat self-indulgent mouth opened at last.

'You see,' he grunted, 'I come here sometimes because it is my village and I help this man by teaching him English.'

He glanced briefly at the man who had first called me.

'But now I do not live here: I live in Lahore, which is more congenial to my temperament. I am a great friend of European priests in Lahore. They always invite me and I find their company congenial, so I go . . . I have just received a certificate first class for bible studies.'

The villager gazed admiringly at his mentor, awed by his education. It was a sad sight and I walked off at a pace that soon had me soaked with perspiration.

After an hour I began to wonder if there was not something I could jettison from my rucksack to lighten my load, and just then a string of three camels appeared. How pleasant it would be, I mused, to have my rucksack carried for me.

I exchanged greetings with the three men accompanying the camels.

'Salaam alaikam' (peace be on thee).

'Wa alaikam ussallam' (and on thee be peace).

'Why don't you put your rucksack on one of the camels?' suggested one of the men. A moment later the leading camel was protesting protractedly with grunts and wheezes—it could not make any other sound because it was muzzled—as my rucksack was tied to its saddle, and within the minute I was a member of the small camel train bound for the outskirts of Gujrat to get loads of stones for the roadworks at Lalamusa.

The great animals' pace never varied as they plodded slowly forward on their floor-polisher feet, their heads just clearing the branches of the trees and so remote from their feet that it appeared they must tumble into ruts and ditches. For some miles, for the novelty of it, I rode on a camel, but the men, who were lean and looked very tough, preferred to walk.

Our pace was the true pace of the Grand Trunk Road, slow and reflective, disturbing nothing; even birds sitting in low branches of the trees above us did not fly away as we passed. The occasional car or lorry on the broad central road seemed to go by on another plane. We passed a herdsman who stood motionless, leaning on his stick as he watched his buffaloes grazing, and everyone was silent until we were almost by, when the last man mumbled 'Salaam alaikam' and the herdsman's reply sounded like the rumble of distant thunder. We were passing through the heart of the wheatlands which provided so many recruits to the old British Indian Army; this was the land of the famous Punjabi Mussulmans, a race of men who bore themselves with pride and dignity. A warm greeting from such men would be like a salute of guns. My companions, too, had a natural dignity. They were obviously poor, living by patient toil as did the cultivators of small plots of land, and for less reward, but they appeared strangers to discontent: the sun shone from a blue sky, the water was good, their Baluchi camels would bring them a bare livelihood; what more, they seemed to say, could a man want? The notion that one may get rich quickly, the optimism of lottery ticket buyers, even the concept that one may by effort provide for a moderately comfortable old age, were unknown to them. Life was no faster than the seasons, and as regular; what mattered was prayer and the rains. They were puzzled that I should concern myself with such things as the names of birds. We parted near the outskirts of Gujrat, where they crossed the main road and turned onto a dusty track between the wheatfields, and I kept on the Grand Trunk Road for the town.

The layout of the town of Gujrat had been determined by its situation, lying as it did in the direct line of march of conquerors of the subcontinent. Long before the British rebuilt the Grand Trunk Road, Gujrat was a fortified and very congested city. It was built on and around a hill, and was once guarded by a stout outer wall. At the summit was a fort built by Akbar, and the town's buildings clustered round this for security, the houses of the richest merchants being nearest the fort's walls. The streets were very narrow and the buildings tall, because no-one was going to venture living outside the city walls in pre-British days.

British officials had lived in the Civil Lines, a long finger pointing from the brown huddle of the city into the flat, green surrounding country. Here stood the tall and impressive Anglican church, its garden still well-tended; the commodious bungalows of past deputy commissioners and other administrative staff; and at the very end of the Lines, against open fields lay the dak bungalow, a square yellow building that rose from the baked red earth like an iced cake.

Dak (literally 'Post') bungalows are still an institution on the subcontinent. Built in the days of British rule they were intended for the use of travelling officials, and provided all the basic comforts that officials staying for a few days would need. Of course, an official in those days travelled with a retinue of servants who would create the comforts of home. It was easy to imagine the arrival of an officer in the early days of the century—the bark of the officer's khitmagar (butler), the unloading of the horses, the attentive chowkidar, the shouting, the banging of doors, and the frantic sweeping and dusting, all very impressive and no doubt very gratifying to the ego of the officer concerned, and all in great contrast to my own arrival. The boy in the tonga that brought me from the Grand Trunk Road argued bitterly about the fare, and having settled with him I walked up the drive with my rucksack on my back. Two unfriendly dogs bounded towards me barking so loudly that any but a deaf chowkidar should have appeared immediately, but no-one did, until I added my voice to that of the dogs, and then a sleepy-looking young Pathan emerged from the servants' quarters to say that this was the chowkidar's day off, but that I could have a room. At dak bungalows any passing traveller is entitled to a room providing it is unoccupied; bookings are not normally taken in advance by some distant official as is the case with PWD bungalows and Civil Resthouses.

The dak bungalow was divided into four equal suites or, as they were termed, sets. Each set had one great room about twenty foot in height, furnished with a cotton-tape bed, a cupboard, four cane chairs, a table, a fan and an electric light, and in addition, for each set, there was a pantry and beyond this a bathroom. Each one had access to two of the four verandahs round the house, and the sets had intercommunicating doors, so that the whole building could if necessary be used by the same party. My set would have accommodated a family of six quite comfortably. After some minutes, when the dust and the sparrows raised by my arrival had had time to resettle I realized that though the place had obviously been neglected for some years, it was potentially a 'desirable residence'. Its main qualifications were that it was large and that it offered privacy; one could easily ignore the plaster peeling from the walls, the dirty carpet, and the dust.

The mali (gardener) entered to say that during the absence of the chowkidar he was in charge, and he tried to make me comfortable by chasing clouds of dust about the room with a dirty rag without, however, catching any. He was a gangling fellow of about twenty-five, with protruding eyes and very large hands and feet, and he smiled zealously. When I asked whether I could have dinner at the dak bungalow he shrugged deprecatingly: the chowkidar was generally the cook, and in his absence no supplies of food were held.

It was now past 8 pm and the prospect of returning the mile or more along the pitch-black road to the nearest bazaar was not attractive, but without food since breakfast my stomach was making a sound like boiling mudpools. The mali came in again half an hour later, apparently after a change of heart. He could, if required, provide breakfast. On being pressed he admitted that he could also prepare a modest dinner. He would personally cook me eggs, he would ride to the bazaar now on his bicycle and buy the eggs for me. His eyes dilating with enthusiasm he asked for a rupee for the eggs.

An hour and a quarter later he stumbled in, smiling modestly and bearing an enormous wooden tray that looked as if it had recently been used for transporting seedlings. Shreds of filthy bandage hung from his right hand over and into the food as he set the table and then with an expression of happy anticipation he stood behind my chair.

It is surprising what can be done with just two eggs and a little flour and water by the application of imagination and culinary skill, or by the complete absence of either. The two 'fried eggs' were now presented like a lurid ceramic and the single chuppatti was nearly half an inch thick. The mali stayed by my side during the meal, moving a glass here, shifting a fork there, whole-heartedly playing the part of waiter. As the coup de grâce he produced a jug of water and a tall, fairly clean glass. Being very thirsty I straightaway took a draught, my mind registering at the moment of drinking the fact that the mali had not brought a glass with him when he came with the meal and had not left the room since then—but the thought came too late. He had used the glass that had stood on the mantel-shelf and had probably lain there untouched for months until polished up on the mali's shirt—he had no other cloth with him. The water had a strong brackish flavour and I recalled advice given me only the previous evening by a commercial traveller in Jhelum, an old hand at dak bungalows, that one should always smell a glass before drinking from it.

When the mali left, the electricity failed and mosquitoes settled on me for the night.

Three hours of rain early next day settled the dust in the narrow lanes of Gujrat. The old town walls had nearly disappeared and now that defence was not the main consideration for town planning, pressure on the centre was being eased by the demolition of some of the oldest buildings. One could still see, however, the defensive pattern of old Gujrat. Each mohalla, or ward, in the town was built so that it could be defended, and was capable of being sealed off from its neighbouring wards by tall stout doors.

Within each ward the lanes were so narrow that in some places two people could not pass at the same time, and these narrow ways could be commanded from the rooftops. Water being vital for defence, each ward had its own well, some of them enormous shafts sunk in Akbar's day and lined with the thin bricks of that time.

Gujrat had often been sacked and had recovered, but the scars from the cataclysm of Partition were still showing nearly twenty-three years after the event. Hindu families who had once been an integral part of the fabric of the town had all gone, much of their property had been destroyed and if their houses had not been razed, they had become homes for refugees. Many of the Hindus had evidently been persons of substance, and among the tall gaunt houses there was still the occasional fine façade, with delicate stone-work and sometimes a sumptuously carved door.

The best view of the town was from the rooftops, which offered exciting possibilities for an agile youngster to climb from one end of the town to the other without once touching the ground. Many of the houses had a pigeon loft on their roofs, and an instrument that looked like a lacrosse net usually lay somewhere nearby: pigeon racing was a popular local sport, and the nets were used for a recognized form of piracy, the capture of rival birds. Another popular roof-top sport was the flying of kites.

Kite-flying combined the graceful art of actually manoeuvring the kite with the thrills of rock-climbing, and enthusiasts gaily dared the heights as their kites engaged in a constant battle in the air. The object was to bring other kites down by cutting their strings, the teeth for the purpose being the ground glass preparation with which the kite twine had been treated. Before Independence it was common for merchants throughout India to tie currency notes below their kites as prize money, but this is now rarely done outside Lucknow.

The roof-tops belonged to children and the children made the biggest impact everywhere in the town. They surrounded me wherever I went, asking questions, demanding to be photographed, chanting, singing and laughing. By the time they were fifteen they all seemed to have the ambition to study at university. The thoughts of the men, however, were on war rather than education, and having been invited to rest in the shop of a seller of fruit cordials, I was soon involved with his friends in a discussion of the Kashmir problem.

'Pakistan cannot be a wholesome entity while the Kashmir problem remains unsolved,' said one man ferociously. 'We, the people who succeeded to Pakistan must settle this problem: why should we expect our children to fight? They would hardly think well of us, their fathers, if we did. For whatever we do they might not reward us by placing flowers on our graves when we die, but at least we must ensure that they don't piss on our graves.' The others nodded their agreement.

The two great issues that fired men's minds in Pakistan were progress and the Kashmir problem. The former was receiving impetus from many foreign aid programmes, with the building of factories and the construction of irrigation works; the latter was a festering sore that left people bewildered and resentful and which impeded national progress by diverting thought and energy from essential daily needs.

Pakistani hospitality, however, remained unimpaired by the various national problems. Wherever I went in Gujrat I was invited to drink tea, to sit and rest awhile, to eat a meal, and I was no sooner on the Grand Trunk Road at the outskirts of the town the next morning, setting out for Lahore, than a bus braked in front of me, though I had not signalled it, and when I came aboard the conductor waived payment and said: 'We are giving you a lift to Lahore.'

Grateful as I was for the ride I could not help observing that the bus appeared to have been designed with the object of preventing the escape of passengers. The doors were very narrow, the windows were small and barred, and the roof was so low that in conjunction with the absence of springs it conspired to bludgeon the will to be free. It was difficult to see anything of the countryside we passed through, the Rechna Doab, the land between the Chenab and the Ravi rivers, but as compensation traditional landscapes showing lakes and mountains, chaste minars and poplar trees, had been painted in bright colours on the interior of the bus.

Bus stations on main routes in the subcontinent can be nearly as exciting as railway stations, with the same clamour of fruit, pan and cigarette vendors, and the same disorderly rush by the ticket grille to get tickets—or if tickets can be bought from the conductor, then the same scramble to board the vehicle. The bus stopped at one such place on the way to Lahore, and among those who boarded was a spruce young man who stood behind the driver's seat, and started a harangue in a stentorian voice, like a prophet of doom. Producing bottles of lotion and boxes of pills from a canvas bag and waving these about, he casually mentioned the sum of one rupee. Boxes and bottles were distributed among passengers sitting at the front while he assured those at the back—he looked fixedly at me—that they too would have a chance to obtain these cure-alls, if they but bided their time in patience. No-one at the rear evinced any interest, nor did he have any success in front, but he had deserved better than failure. His pitch had great emotional power and had he operated in a better market he would have done well for himself.

After another bumpy ride the bus rattled at last over the bridge across the River Ravi and into Lahore.

4

Lahore, like Gujrat to its north, had developed as a fortified city. It was in the direct line of march of freebooters from beyond the Khyber, of men who, like Ahmed Shah Abdali, sacked the city not once, but several times.

That Lahore not only survived, but managed to prosper between incursions, and was even successful on occasion at beating away invaders, testifies to the resilience of Lahorias, and the strength of the walls they built.

A city today of one and a half million people, Lahore sprawls across the plain with broad, dusty roads leading to new housing estates well beyond the perimeter of the city as it was in British days, and far from the tight-knit square mile of alleys and tall secretive buildings that was the old walled city.

It was old Lahore and the Anarkali bazaar area south of it leading to the museum and Charing Cross that Kipling wrote about in several short stories, and in *Kim*. Kipling was mentioned in the tourist brochure I had acquired. 'The cavalcades of kings, the fancies of queens and the ambitions of princes have all paid tributes to their love for Lahore', it stated, 'and even that inveterate Englishman Rudyard Kipling lost his heart to Lahore and settled down here for a lifetime.'

A slight exaggeration: Kipling was born in Bombay, educated in England, and came out to Lahore in 1882, a week before his seventeenth birthday. His father was curator of Lahore museum, and the young Kipling became assistant editor of the *Civil and Military Gazette*. He was only twenty-one when he left to join the *Pioneer* in Allahabad, and he left India in 1889. Lahore had already featured in a number of his short stories and later, in *Kim,* he wrote of the 'wonderful walled city', where Kim was 'hand in glove with men who led lives stranger than anything Haroun al Raschid dreamed of', and where Kim himself 'lived in a life wild as that of the *Arabian Nights*'.

One approach to the old city is from the railway station, along the Landa Bazaar, a narrow way bordered by flimsy stalls. In Kipling's day the Landa Bazaar had been the site of the serai of Muhammad Sultan, much frequented by horse-dealers, and the original perhaps for the 'Kashmir Serai' patronized by Mahbub Ali in *Kim*.

A beggar in a long grey robe, jingling anklets and wearing what looked like a snake-charmer's implements suspended about his neck, strode through the bazaar, thrusting a small metal bucket under each stall-holder's nose but receiving little for his pains. Judging from the performance of other beggars in Lahore, this one's technique was faulty, his main defect as a beggar being that he looked too healthy. The exhibition of deformities is the basis for begging in Lahore today, not the facial play and wit relied on by the beggars with whom Kim consorted near the Taksali Gate and of whom he remarked: 'Those who beg in silence, starve in silence.'

Landa Bazaar ends by the Delhi Gate, one of the thirteen gates into the old walled city of Lahore. The original walls had been built between 1584 and 1598 by the Emperor Akbar, but these had fallen into decay and had been almost completely rebuilt by Ranjit Singh, the great Sikh ruler of the Punjab, at the beginning of the nineteenth century. What remains now of these walls is in poor repair. The Delhi Gate on the eastern side of the city still stands, white and rather dilapidated, and I passed through it into the old city. It was as congested, busy and vigorous as London must have been in the sixteenth century.

Tongas, heavy-laden with black burqua'd women, tried to pass bullock-carts loaded with sacks of flour, threatening the little stores on either side of the narrow lane. Above the stores the houses were tall, narrow and secretive, vouchsafing no glimpse of life beyond their walls. Here and there the way opened onto areas where sellers of fruit and vegetables foregathered, and where the sun shone through. But the sun could not penetrate the lanes. The mosque of Wazir Khan stands in a fairly open square, a blaze of light and colour compared with all around it, its tiled minarets glowing in the sun. Its walls are covered with brilliantly-coloured, glazed tiles, with motifs of flowers and intertwining leaves in yellows and greens and pinks and blues. Above the entrance is written in Persian characters: 'Remove thy heart from the gardens of the world, and know that this building is the true abode of man.'

A few steps beyond the mosque and one is in the labyrinthine world of shadows again, where separate traders have their own lanes, sellers of meat in one lane (or 'galli'), bakers in another, beaters of silver, who make fine silver-leaf sweet decorations, in their own enclave, and goldsmiths along a broader, more prosperous way; each lane has its own peculiar features, and the whole area has a distinctly medieval character.

Lahore fort at the northern tip of the city was built by the Moghuls and certainly performed its function, but although its walls are battered, it is now being maintained as a showpiece. It was in this fort that the British formally annexed the Punjab and took possession of the Koh-i-Nur (Mountain of Light) diamond. The Koh-i-Nur and the Peacock throne had been part of the booty taken away by Nadir Shah, the Persian, after he sacked Delhi in 1739. After his assassination it came into the hands of Ahmed Shah Abdali, ruler of Afghanistan and a great harrier of Hindustan, and it was from his grandson, Shah Shuja, that Maharajah Ranjit Singh, greatest of Sikh rulers, acquired it. Ten years after Ranjit Singh's death and following two Anglo-Sikh wars, his son, Maharajah Dalip Singh, handed over the Koh-i-Nur to the British and stepped down from his father's throne.

Near the fort is the Badshahi mosque, built in the time of the Emperor Aurangzeb, and from its lofty southern minarets one looks down over the Hira Mandi.

Hira Mandi means, literally, the Jewel Market, but ask any man where it is and he grins. The jewels are of an unusual sort, especially in a country with a somewhat repressive attitude to women. For this is the area where Lahore's 'dancing girls', or, as is written in *Kim,* 'the Harpies who paint their eyes and trap the stranger', are to be found.

In the old days many of the girls who provided very private entertainment in the purlieus of Hira Mandi had been trained as singers and dancers and were considerable artists, much in demand among the wealthy, who hired them in the main for an evening of musical entertainment, and by whom they were sometimes given substantial sums of money or jewellery. In the old days too, nawabs would send their daughters to the more famous of the ladies of Hira Mandi to learn deportment and the arts of conversation. Some of the inhabitants of Hira Mandi, however, had no high pretensions and their services were simply of the sort more likely to be in demand among caravaneers who had not seen a woman for months.

Today, it is said, Hira Mandi no longer has the patronage of the nawabs and appeals more to the middle and lower classes, but it is still a lively area.

Although prostitution is now officially banned in Pakistan, lean and furtive men were conducting a sales and public relations campaign on passers-by on behalf of their clients, promising immense delight for very moderate sums. Officially though, all the girls are now dancing girls or singers, and one can hire a girl and a local group, for an evening or a shorter period, to watch an unsophisticated dance or hear the latest songs from the films.

As I passed through the gap in the crumbling city wall that is called the Taksali Gate, I heard the sound of a mandolin and of singing, and though it was only early afternoon, small clusters of girls with boldly painted faces—they looked very young—were already abroad, looking at passers-by. As foreign visitors have always been rare in the Hira Mandi I received very flattering attention.

Prakash Tandon mentions the Hira Mandi in his book *Punjabi Century* and, reminiscing about the area in the late 1920s, writes of: 'Jasmine tinted Kashmirans, wheat-skinned Punjabans, grey-eyed Paharans, delicately modelled Delhiwallis, taut and proud-looking Rajasthanis, the occasional hawk-faced Baluch or a rosy, blue-eyed Pathani. They came from all over the north, from the mountain passes of Karakorum to the hills of Kumaon, from the Nagin of Srinagar to the lakes of Udaipur, dressed in their different clothes and hair-styles.'

Today there are still flashes of colour in Hira Mandi, and wandering through the narrow ways is to go back in a time-machine to the Middle Ages. At night the police patrol Hira Mandi in pairs and wear steel helmets and the atmosphere of mystery takes on an extra quality of menace.

On the south side of Old Lahore is the Lohari Gate, perhaps the busiest entrance to the city because it faces Anarkali Bazaar, the main channel between old and modern Lahore. The approaches to the gate are lined with restaurants famous for their kulfi (ice-cream), with stalls of flower-sellers and garland-makers, the shops of chemists and booksellers, the shanties of newspaper-sellers, who sell paper by weight, and with the sheds of horse-fodder vendors, who cater for the tonga horses which are stabled at night in nearby sheds.

Modern Lahore begins beyond Anarkali, by the Punjab University and the Museum, the 'Ajaib Gher', which still contains the

7 In the Golden Temple, Amritsar

8 Farmer near the River Beas in the Punjab

famous Buddhist relics that so fascinated Kim's Lama. Zam Zammah, 'Kim's Gun', still stands at the west of the Mall, a mighty piece of artillery, and four boys sat astride it, as Kim had done, 'in defiance of municipal orders.'

Across the road a heap of old clothes resolved itself into a long-haired old man wearing a loose grey robe reaching to his feet, and strings of beads of different sizes, shapes and colours around his neck. He was that interesting survival from past days and symbol of the subcontinent, a snake-charmer; the fact that he was the first of that tribe I had seen on this trip suggested that snake-charmers were dwindling in numbers. It was evident from his excitement on seeing me that tourists were rare at this time of the year. He blew a dolorous note on his gourd pipe as I approached and sharply tapped the wicker basket at his feet, doubtless to wake the cobra that lay curled within. I could not have passed him: too many people were drawing in with looks of expectation on their faces and I could not disappoint them, and anyway, I have always been fascinated by the showmanship of snake-charmers. He started by demanding five rupees as the price for starting the performance.

'Nonsense,' I ejaculated, and sheered away. He advanced on me waving his arms.

'Three rupees,' he said. The crowd, which was rapidly gathering around us, laughed as one man.

'That's a ridiculous price,' I complained.

'Shame,' remonstrated an elderly man with a fine grey beard, 'The show isn't worth an anna. He's trying to rob you. Don't give him anything.' Other members of the audience rebuked the snake-charmer for his cupidity.

'Two rupees,' he moaned, his eyes bright and sharp in his old head.

'Eight annas,' I offered firmly, and he set to with alacrity, pushing back his robe and squatting by the basket. He piped perfunctorily, but music appeared to have little meaning for the snake, which after the basket lid was raised only moved when its master struck the basket. The dark metallic head rose as if on a weak spring, and swayed slightly, a sinister object because of its disciplined control of the obvious tensile strength in its coils. The tempo of the music made no difference to the snake's movements, and it was clearly a sop for the audience. The show was soon over; the snake-charmer showed no signs of being enthusiastic about the size of his audience; he only expected payment from me and he was right. When I had paid my eight annas the crowd dispersed, including the policeman who had come with the notion of clearing the footpath, but stayed for the performance.

I was staying at the opposite end of Lahore from the old walled city, in a youth hostel which must have been an impressive building when it was opened, but now needed considerable attention from a good handyman. The men's dormitory was in the basement and we were all locked in there at 10 pm each night by the warden, perhaps to prevent us wandering upstairs to the women's dormitory.

In the early morning and evening I would drink tea and eat at a nearby café where the sweets were kept in an impressive glass case, and it was some time before I noticed that the boy in charge usually left the case open and that the 'jilaybees' and 'luddoos' and delicious 'gulab jamans' were battened upon in their shelter by flies. When I did discover this I decided it was too late to worry. The little boy in the shop had fine features and large eyes ringed with 'kajal'—the deposit on a lamp-globe left after burning mustard oil, used for the dual purpose of eye ointment and decoration. He had a very languid manner, was offhand to customers and paid little heed to the man who seemed to be the owner, a stolid middle-aged fellow whose actions were very deliberate and who would not be hurried. I wondered at the latter's indulgence towards this rather pretty boy until another customer, indicating the man and the boy, illustrated their relationship with graphic gestures, and the boy, observing this, reacted by smiling and stretching like a satisfied cat.

Politics hamper so many travel opportunities. Following the India-Pakistan war of 1965, the thirty-four mile stretch of the Grand Trunk Road between Lahore and Amritsar had been closed, and it was still not possible to travel along this sector. One now had to make a detour through Kasur and Ferozepore, and the journey from Lahore to Amritsar took a whole day.

First a bus to Kasur, then a tonga to the border at Hussainiwala.

What a tonga it was. It lacked any vestige of paint, as did all the tongas on the border run; the woodwork was cracked, the metal-work was twisted and the canopy tilted weakly to one side. The wheels were strong enough, indeed they looked as though they could have carried a bullock-cart, but I was apprehensive about the axle. The horse, poor animal, appeared only just able to stand upon its feet, and then only because it was held up by the shafts. The driver could well have said with the cabman in *Pickwick Papers*: '... when he's in it, we bears him up werry tight, and takes him in werry short, so as he can't werry well fall down; and we've got a pair o' precious large wheels on, so ven he does move, they run after him and he must go on—he can't help it.'

Another passenger on this tonga was a conciliatory greybeard from Uttar Pradesh in India, who did not remonstrate even when the canopy collapsed on him for a second time. The horse and I both thought the tonga grossly overloaded with just two passengers, but we had not long left Kasur when we had to turn back for an additional load. We had been commandeered by a sergeant of the border police ('Assistant Emigration Officer' was the designation he gave himself), who insisted that three enormous sacks of flour be taken aboard, provisions for the border colony. My protests had no effect, the sacks were loaded, but the sergeant was punished by having to work nearly as hard as the horse. The poor animal was in no condition to pull such a load and whenever it stopped, which was after every hundred yards or so, the tonga pulled back into the thick, dusty verge of the road and the sergeant, who was following on a bicycle, had to dismount and push the tonga wheel while the tonga-wallah hauled at the bridle, to get the vehicle under way again. Meanwhile my fellow passenger and I sat tight.

At the border a Pakistani customs official was morosely sniffing some files. 'You see we have had these stored in a godown, together with confiscated goods, and they smell of opium.'

I sniffed at the files but could smell nothing. Perhaps it was a trap. On the Indian side of the border I was received with great goodwill by grinning Sikhs, and a grizzled sergeant shook me by the hand and summoned a cycle-rickshaw to take me to Ferozepore station.

5

India . . . I was in a new country, but there was little change in the countryside, for this was still the wheatbelt of the subcontinent, the Punjab, the Land of the Five Rivers.

An immediately noticeable difference, however, was in the people. As to size, there was nothing in it; the Punjabis, whether in Pakistan or India, are a big race, but the Sikhs, the predominant group in the Indian Punjab, are easily distinguishable by their beards and turbans. What was even more noticeable was that women were visible again, and the women of the Punjab are well worth looking at. In Pakistan one does occasionally see women who are unveiled, but this is a comparatively rare occurrence: in Pakistan a woman's place is still very much in the home, she is heard rather than seen, and when she does stir out she usually wears the concealing burqa.

What was less noticeable at the time was that I had entered a land where Hinduism is the dominant religion; when I joined the Grand Trunk Road again I would journey for most of the way to Calcutta through the heartland of the most mystifying of the world's major religions.

It is a religion which, unlike Mohammedanism, Christianity or Buddhism, has no central figure as the interpreter or revealer of divine wisdom, but is derived from the myths and legends and philosophy of a people who more than 3,000 years ago came to India from somewhere beyond the mountains that border the subcontinent in the north.

This was an Aryan people, tall and fair, who entered the country through the traditional north-west gateway in about 1500 BC and in increasing numbers settled throughout northern India, mainly in what is now called the Punjab, before pushing eastward into the Gangetic Plain. They brought with them elaborate rituals for the worship of the powers of Nature, mythical concepts of creation, and prescribed rules for almost all aspects of life, all of which were to be enshrined in the Vedas, the source religious books of the Hindus.

The Vedas were not written down until centuries after the Aryans came to India: they were passed on by word of mouth, the trustees of this formidable repository of religious tradition being the priests. These priests performed another very important function, the conduct of the sacrifices which were an integral part of the Aryan worship and for which extremely complicated rituals were evolved.

It is not surprising that in that early society the priests—the Brahmans—held the highest rank, being followed by warriors, the working class, and beneath all, and almost beneath all notice, the menials. This was to become the basis of the Hindu caste system. In today's India the visitor may not be aware of caste divisions, mainly because the government has made it illegal to discriminate on the grounds of caste, but most Hindus I questioned on the subject agreed that the caste divisions are still the strongest social force in India today: marriages still tend to take place not only between members of the same caste but between members of sub-clans of the same caste.

Gradually the Vedic religion of the Aryans in India absorbed the cultures of others who had entered the country over the centuries as well as those of the Dravidian and other peoples who had been in India when the Aryans arrived: its mythology was expanded and it moved from a position of having no idols at all to the situation as it is today when gods are worshipped in a confusing diversity of forms. The Hindu triad of Brahma the Creator, Vishnu the Preserver and Shiva the Destroyer, were joined in the Hindu pantheon by innumerable incarnations of the gods that had been evolved to suit the needs of many different sorts and conditions of men. All this took time: about 2,000 years. Periodically it was suggested that the Brahmans, who made the Vedas their own special preserve, were deliberately complicating rituals in order to maintain their own importance. The tenets of Buddhism were essentially a reaction against the complexities of Brahmanic worship; the Buddhists opposed the notions of caste and excessive ceremony, and preached that a man gained more merit by his own good deeds than through sacrificial rituals.

Buddhism achieved a dominant position in India in about 300 BC, some two hundred years after the death of the Buddha, and for the next 600 years it was the way of life followed by most of the people in India. The old beliefs and practices had not died, however, and Buddhism in India declined and eventually it all but disappeared from the country. The Brahmans regained their pre-eminent place in society.

It was during the resurgence of the Brahmans, and of a Hinduism that had absorbed many of the Buddhist beliefs, that the Puranas and the great Hindu epics—the Mahabharata and the Ramayana—were written, their fantastic stories of the gods, though often at odds with the Vedas, being absorbed as part of the very fabric of Hinduism. And what made the stories of the gods very palatable to a simple people was the way in which they were represented as living in readily identifiable places in India.

One does not have to browse long amidst Hindu lore to realize how much confusion the mixture of legends and myths and good solid Vedic precept must have caused in the uneducated mind, but whatever its effect on the masses might have been, the religious heritage of Hinduism has given the educated Hindu a mind that is extremely agile and flexible. This one discovers on becoming involved in abstract discussions with a Hindu, for he will almost certainly be able to develop the most sophisticated of arguments from the most unpromising of premises. He will also be able to quote chapter and verse from a number of religious works in order to suit his case.

An old school teacher from Delhi who was waiting for a train at Ferozepore station smiled when I asked him whether it was known how many gods were worshipped by the Hindus today, and said: 'All the waters that fall from the sky into the rivers go ultimately to the sea, and similarly, worship of all the gods reaches the one supreme god . . . Keshav.'

I would have enjoyed travelling with him but his train was not my train. The journey from Ferozepore to Amritsar was a long slow one, without the interest of a journey along a main line, and the train finally steamed into Amritsar at 1.30 am, not an hour at which many people would care to arrive in a strange city.

And Amritsar, I decided the moment I stepped out of the light of the platform, looked extremely sinister.

Two black-bearded rickshaw men were waiting in the silent station yard, white teeth glowing in the faint light from the booking hall, faces screaming menace. At that lonely hour it seemed essential to establish some relationship with these spectres, and I managed this by arguing about the fare to the 'nearest clean hotel'.

Somewhere in the dark city, where no single light shone, my rickshaw-wallah stopped outside a tall bolted door and hammered at it until all Amritsar should have woken. But Amritsar was dead and so it seemed was the watchman. The door was opened at last, however, and a smooth-faced youth who spoke fluent English led me up rickety stairs to a room somewhere near the roof. The curtains hung crazily, the lavatory was filthy, the atmosphere close and the bed dirty, but little remained of the night.

Amritsar is the spiritual home of the Sikhs, the site of the Golden Temple, most sacred of Sikh shrines, and the great majority of the population of the city are Sikhs. Across the border, in Lahore in Pakistan, I had not seen a single Sikh, though the city had been capital of a Sikh Empire in the first half of the nineteenth century: the chaos during the Mutiny in 1857 was on a small scale compared with the bloody upheavals of Partition in 1947. Sikhism is a relatively new religion among the many religions of India. It grew from the teachings of Guru Nanak, a Hindu by birth, who in the early sixteenth century tried to bridge the gap between Moslem and Hindu theology. The religious principles that he formulated became very popular with the farming community of the Punjab and later received encouragement from the Moghul Emperor Akbar. The number of Sikhs grew rapidly. Akbar's successors, Jehangir, Shah Jehan and especially Aurangzeb, were, however, less tolerant and the Sikhs frequently became hunted men. Gradually the Sikh community took to arms, developing a cavalry force that specialized in hit-and-run tactics.

The Sikhs were dedicated as a fighting force at a macabre ceremony on the first day of spring (Baisakh) in 1699. Thousands of Sikhs had assembled that day at the request of Guru Gobind, tenth in the line of Sikh spiritual leaders, and after conducting a service the Guru looked down upon the congregation, drew his sword and demanded five men for sacrifice.

One man stepped forward and was taken into a tent, and moments later the Guru stepped out, his sword dripping blood. A second man rose and he too was taken into the tent, and again the Guru emerged with dripping sword. In turn two more men went in and the Guru came out as before. Then the fifth man went in, but this time, instead of emerging alone, the Guru came out with the five doughty souls who had offered themselves for sacrifice. Five goats had been killed in their stead.

The five men were baptized as founder members of the Khalsa

('The Pure'). Henceforth, said Guru Gobind Singh, all Sikhs—'disciples'—would be called 'Singh', a word derived from the Sanskrit for 'lion'.

'Until now', he told the assembled Sikhs, 'you have all been saints. Now you will be warriors too.'

He instructed them to observe five rules of appearance: hair and beards should be kept unshorn; a comb should be kept in the hair to ensure good grooming; a steel bangle should be worn at the wrist as a constant reminder that the Sikhs were now a fighting sect; a kirpan (a curved sword) should be carried; and knee-length underwear, of the type worn by soldiers at that time, should be worn.

And so to the religious dicta of the gurus was added the warlike mien that still characterizes the majority of Sikhs today, although the kirpan is now worn only by Nihangs, the elite among Sikh forces.

The history of the Punjab in the eighteenth century is largely a narrative of battles in which the Sikhs were involved, first against the Moghul armies, and later against Afghan marauders. At the end of the century a Sikh became Maharajah of the Punjab, and for fifty years a Sikh monarch ruled the Punjab until this territory was annexed by the British. Since then the Sikhs have always provided a considerable proportion of the soldiers in the armies of India.

The Sikhs have also spread throughout northern India as traders, and are pre-eminent in the mechanical trades. The Punjab, though, is still the home of most Sikhs, and here they farm most of the land in the State.

Today they form a prosperous community, but as any visitors to Amritsar will be aware, young Sikhs of today are not being allowed to forget the battles and the bloodshed of the past.

The major Sikh shrine, the Durbar Sahib ('Golden Temple'), is in the centre of Amritsar. It is surrounded by bazaars where the number of men dressed in blue robes, with blue and yellow turbans ringed with sharp steel quoits and armed with swords and spears, might well cause a visitor to believe that he is near the centre of an army preparing for battle. These men are Nihangs, members of a special cadre of Sikh fighters that developed as a counter movement to the Moslem Ghazis, a body of men regarded as suicide squads, who were reputed never to turn aside from any objective.

Tall gaunt men with spears guard the entrances to the Golden Temple and to the nearby serai for pilgrims.

Every Sikh temple provides free accommodation for pilgrims (and free food too), as many a wanderer from Europe has discovered. At Amritsar the accommodation is a serai with 156 rest rooms, and there, after having been scrutinized by an old warrior at the gate, I was given a room furnished with a charpai.

The Ram Das Serai, named after the fourth Guru of the Sikhs—the founder of Amritsar—was as busy as a large railway station, with much packing and spreading out of provisions. Here, a family was preparing breakfast over a paraffin stove; there, an old man sat with hands clasped and prayed aloud; here, a Sikh tied his turban, and there a girl standing on the verandah combed long black hair that fell over her blue silk blouse. A few people were stretched out on the verandah floor. Indians have the ability to stretch out almost anywhere, quite unselfconsciously, and sleep; on bare floors, on the streets, on railway platforms, in temples, railway carriages, museums. The atmosphere in the serai was one of delightful informality, but the severe-looking guardian at the gate was a reminder that most people were here on a pilgrimage to the holiest shrine of a martial race.

Guards kept watch at the temple entrances too, and their surveillance was oppressive, but fortunately I was introduced to the temple by a guide who ensured that I transgressed no rules—that I wore a hat, that I removed my shoes and washed my feet before entering the temple precincts. An inner courtyard paved with marble surrounds the holy tank, the pool of nectar—'Amrit'—from which Amritsar takes its name, and the heart of the temple is at the end of a causeway in the centre of the pool.

The water in the tank reflects the white marble and the gilt domes of the temple and here, as in many other places in India, one is aware of the great skill with which water is used as part of an architectural concept where one's surroundings are designed to assist contemplation. Most of the visitors to the temple were old men with silky white beards, and many elders served at water fountains and in the 'langar'—the free kitchen.

In contrast to this picture of tranquillity, a museum within the temple precincts reminds worshippers of insults of the past. Large paintings re-create the deaths of Sikh martyrs and desecrations of the Golden Temple are enumerated with supporting photographic evidence of such occasions within recent years. It is a sombre place, that museum, and I was to think of it later when I visited Sirhind, an example of how thorough Sikh vengeance could be.

A number of beggars circulated among the pilgrims in the bazaar outside the temple, and when I set off towards the Grand Trunk Road next day three plump beggars in saffron robes, carrying the usual gourd begging bowls, stood in my way. When I offered one of them four annas (a quarter of a rupee) he laughed derisively.

'No, no,' he roared, 'not that. Five rupees.'

They followed me down the lane, bargaining it seems, and the last I heard as I passed out of earshot were demands for three rupees.

The Grand Trunk Road passes through the outskirts of Amritsar, and I walked for over an hour before the countryside was in sight and soon after that I was passing through some of the richest farmland in India. After I had walked some miles and my rucksack seemed to have become appreciably heavier, I asked for a ride on a bullock-cart, and making myself comfortable on a pile of kikar logs, instantly fell asleep. The carters awoke me more than an hour later when they were about to turn into a side road.

Punjabis are a sociable race and love to travel over short distances. Bus stations in the Punjab are meeting points for friends and every little settlement and village near a bus route has its teahouse and sweetstall. Whenever I stopped I would be surrounded by tall, curious Sikhs. 'Where are you going?' was the first question I expected, and then 'Where have you come from?', 'Are you a student?', 'What are your qualifications?', 'Are you in business or in service?', 'What is your designation?', 'Are you travelling alone?'.

The Sikh greeting is 'Sat Sri Akal', meaning literally 'God is good', and these are helpful words to know in the Punjab. The Sikh policeman on duty at a village I came to in the late afternoon told me to sit at a teahouse and rest: he would stop a lorry for me. I heard him telling those waiting for a bus that here was a foreigner who spoke Punjabi and had greeted him with 'Sat Sri Akal'.

My destination that night was Dhilwan, a village on the eastern bank of the river Beas, just off the Grand Trunk Road, thirty miles from Amritsar. On a previous visit to Delhi I had been given a letter of introduction to a Mr Butalia, a medical officer at the Dhilwan Primary Health Centre, and though I normally like to leave matters to chance when I am travelling, Mr Butalia's brother in Delhi had talked so enthusiastically about the countryside around Dhilwan, the country in which he was reared, that I was delighted to have the opportunity to stay there.

A truck, stopped for me by the policeman, took me as far as the river Beas, and I then walked down a side road into silence, an ant on the plain. A pair of blue jays started from a tree and flew away chattering noisily, disturbing a pair of rose-ringed parakeets that gave a short and noisy aerial performance before returning to their trees. A Sikh cultivator appeared from the midst of a field of barley, and then a mushroom of smoke arose and Dhilwan station on the Delhi-Amritsar line came into view. The large village of Dhilwan was a mile and a half further on, at the end of a long avenue of mango and jaman trees, and I arrived there at dusk slightly worried about presenting my letter of introduction so late in the day.

Mr Jangbhir Butalia had not been advised by his brother of my possible arrival, for Indian hospitality is as casual as it is embracing, but when I asked for Jangbhir Singh at the Primary Health Centre I was treated like a visiting monarch. My rucksack was taken from me and I was led to Jangbhir's house where I was welcomed very hospitably. I was receiving one of the benefits of the great Indian joint family system. Indians rarely pay for accommodation when they travel as they usually manage to stay with a relative or the friend of a relative. In a country of large families, where even a third cousin is a near relative, the advantages of such a system are obvious. I was accepted as one of the family.

The Primary Health Centre at Dhilwan was the medical centre for Block Nadala, an area comprising 151 villages with a total population of 100,000, and the young doctor in charge, a woman, was the only person capable of performing minor surgery. Mr Butalia, a tall Sikh about thirty years old, was her second in command. The other senior staff were the family planning educator, and the sanitary inspector. The family planning educator, Kunder Singh, was a slim Sikh with waxed mustachios who had the gravity of one whose work is recognized to be 'of the utmost importance'. The Sanitary Inspector, Mr Rajandass, was a fierce little man of military bearing, who had the heavy responsibility for eradicating all communicable diseases in the Block.

During dinner at Mr Butalia's house the men discussed their jobs. Mr Rajandass claimed that the main scourges of the past, smallpox and malaria, had been completely eradicated from the Block, and that cholera and typhoid could be controlled, a success achieved by the combination of methodical vaccination, spraying, and a growing awareness among the local people of the nature of disease and how it may be prevented by better hygiene. A frequent cause of disease had been the unhygienic well, with its common bucket handled by all. Open wells were now being replaced by handpumps, which were fairly cheap to install in this Block near the Beas where water lay between ten and twenty feet below the surface. A handpump here would cost 100 rupees to install, whereas in the Jullundur District, the installation of a pump might cost 500 rupees or more because water lay as much as 120 feet below the surface. Where wells were still used, the water would be disinfected and villagers encouraged to bring their own buckets rather than use a common one. Persuading people of the necessity for vaccination had been more difficult; superstition was a declining force in the community, but it was still there. When, for instance, the Bhakra Dam was built in the Punjab and water was made available to irrigate farms that hitherto had depended entirely on the monsoon, farmers had been advised by local sages not to use the water because all the power had been extracted from it to make electricity, and it would make the soil barren. Education, all the men agreed, was the first task of the medical staff, whether vaccinators, sprayers or men from the dung disposal unit. Education failing, they could have recourse to the law.

'Babies must be vaccinated against smallpox between three and six months,' said Mr Rajandass. 'If parents refuse we try to educate them. If they still refuse we have a writ served on them and they have to appear in Court.'

Kunder Singh said little. He had only recently been promoted to the post of family planning educator, and his Department could not as yet claim much success, though this was not for want of zeal. District midwives and auxiliary nurses spoke to the women, and because family planning was a national programme, Kunder Singh could invoke the assistance of all and any of the men at the Medical Centre in an effort to convert the men in the villages.

'How do you try to convert the men?' I asked.

'We show them condoms,' he said simply.

The meal had just been cleared away and on the centre of the table he laid a government issue French Letter, a long crescent shaped balloon of about the consistency of a rubber glove. We all gazed at it gravely and I wondered what the villagers would make of it. Kunder Singh admitted that few as yet had shown any enthusiasm to be enrolled in the family planning programme, though government propaganda was having an effect amongst the educated; perhaps he regretted that he had not the power of legal compulsion enjoyed by his colleague the vaccinator. It was likely, however, that some villagers would be glad to try the new methods. Malcolm Darling in his book *The Punjab Peasant,* writing about the Punjab some fifty years ago, mentions a Sikh cultivator:

> 'Thirty years of age and the owner of seventeen acres—a substantial holding in the Central Punjab—he had been married eleven years and within the first six years had had two sons and two daughters, and thereafter neither son nor daughter. This, he said, was due to self-restraint and method and to sleeping out by the well on certain days of the month. More sons, he explained, will have no land to cultivate and I do not wish to make beggars of them all!'

The subdivision of property, with fragmentation of separate fields because inheritors cannot agree about their relative value, is one cause of inefficiency in Indian agriculture. This was now being used as a powerful argument for birth control in the Punjab, a province where love of land is perhaps the greatest love of all.

Of serious crime cases in the Punjab, 40 per cent result from disputes over land, 40 per cent from disputes over women, and 20 per cent have other causes.

The price of agricultural land in the district had spiralled, and now fetched around ten thousand rupees—that is about £500—an acre, mainly because Punjabis who had emigrated from there to the UK were returning with money they had earned abroad to buy land and settle down as cultivators, and others were sending out money to relatives for the purchase of land, the installation of tube-wells, and the purchase of tractors and fertilizers. Land is life for the Punjabi peasant, though members of the new generation are going in increasing numbers into business or service in the cities.

Next morning a cool breeze rustled in the mango trees and the sun shone from a pale blue sky over fields stretching to the warmth under a faint early morning mist. Men were busy at the pumps or returning from their toilet in the fields, carrying brass water jars. Smoke rose from dung fires in the flat-roofed houses and some cultivators were already setting out on their cycles. A policeman standing outside the pink stone thana (police station) stretched and scratched his belly, and the sound of a village at breakfast-time became distinguishable under the dominating beat of sacred music broadcast from the local Sikh gurdwara (place of worship). It was just the hour for setting out on the Grand Trunk Road, but first I was to have breakfast with Mr Butalia.

Mr Butalia had, it appeared, hospitably assumed that I would stay a week and on my arrival at his house declared a general holiday. He, together with Mr Rajandass and Jogbinder Singh, a vaccinator, would show me around the countryside that day. The Health Centre Land Rover was out of action, so we would go by cycle after we had breakfasted and I had been taken round the village.

Dhilwan had recently been electrified by a grid from Bhakra Dam, but the power was extremely weak and as Mr Butalia had lately been to Delhi and had bought a shining new electric kettle that he wanted to use, we were an hour-and-a-half about our tea. Then we were an hour-and-a-half on our leisurely round of the village, chatting to shopkeepers and craftsmen. One of the busiest craftsmen was the maker of charpais, which were sold in parts: the legs cost 50 paise each, the two long bamboo supports cost Rs 2.50 each, the shorter ones Rs 1.50 each and the rope, of which four kilos would be used, cost Rs 1.50 a kilo, so all the materials one needed for making a bed cost a total of Rs 16, less than £1. In a neighbouring shop, a dyer and starcher of turbans was seated between bowls of different coloured liquids; his charges were 4 annas for starching and one rupee for dyeing. The village mistry (carpenter) worked in a yard littered with rough timber and bullock-cart parts. He used shisham and kikar, the common trees of the Punjab countryside, and produced carts of traditional pattern, with great wooden wheels and a minimum of metal. These sold for about Rs 450 (£25) and it was claimed that they would last for at least twenty years.

Dhilwan's main way was a quagmire churned by the heavy wheels of bullock-carts. A sports bicycle would be no good for these scramble conditions, especially if it was to be loaded as the Indians load their machines. A farmer jolted by to market on a bicycle carrying milk in brass urns strapped to the side of the carrier. Another cyclist had a pile of goatskins on his crossbar and carrier, and was taking them to the tanning factory fourteen miles away. An aged postman, wearing a tall khaki turban with a red band, rode in from Beas with an enormous mailbag on his cycle carrier. The bicycles were staid, black, functional and heavy, and when at rest stood on stands similar to those one expects on motor cycles. They cost on average Rs 225 (£12.50) a high price in India, but this was the affluent Punjab and I never saw as many cycles in the other states I visited.

Mr Butalia now returned to his home to make more tea and change his clothes for the bicycle outing and I was surprised to see him wear an immaculate dark pin-stripe suit complete with waistcoat, all hand-tailored of course, as the expense of tailoring is the customer's least worry in India. Mr Jogbinder Singh, the vaccinator, went to borrow the auxiliary nurse's bicycle and while the electric kettle heated we watched three young snake charmers who had started a performance in the cul-de-sac leading to the house. The oldest was not more than fourteen and glared at us balefully out of a face pitted with smallpox scars that Mr Rajandass assured me he would not have had had he lived in the Punjab; these lads were beggar boys from Rajasthan.

The sun was at its zenith when we started out, four men on two machines, Mr Rajandass sitting behind Mr Singh, the vaccinator, and I on the carrier of Mr Butalia's bicycle. I had no confidence either in Mr B or in my ability to stay on the cycle and suffered for this want of faith by a nervous rigidity that brought on a mild cramp to trouble me for days afterwards. Mr Rajandass by contrast showed how it should be done, sitting nonchalantly without holding on, coat folded on his lap and my camera case hanging from his shoulder. He had of course mounted the carrier properly, leaping on when the cycle was moving, while I had clambered aboard when the cycle was stationary. Once under way we became Fast Traffic, scorching past the groaning wagons, herds of cattle and barefooted pedestrians, the two Sikh cyclists bent over the handlebars, turban tops in the wind, while I hoped Mr B would remember when passing anything that my legs were protruding stiffly on one side.

We passed two rabbiters near the Beas, sturdy broad-faced men who, with their deep-chested mongrel dogs, were working the rough uncultivated strip adjoining the road embankment; they looked like the robust and coarse British peasants of mid-eighteenth-century prints. Across the river, tied to a stake in a copse of trees was an elephant, an old listless fellow with filed-off tusks and rheumy eyes, who had jibbed at crossing the bridge and was being left without food until hunger would persuade him to follow his mahout, elephant-driver. He was past the days of labour, and earned his keep by being taken on show round country villages, where people had rarely if ever seen an elephant and where he would be a more popular entertainment than dancing bears, performing monkeys, or the more common cobra and mongoose acts.

We turned off at the township of Beas, near the west bank of the river and were soon in the quiet countryside, the silence disturbed only by the plaintive squeak of a distant chaff-cutter, the cough of a tube-well motor, and the agitation of parrots. Smoke on the horizon showed where gur, the rough local sugar made from sugar cane, was being prepared, and a flurry of distant black dots, seemingly as small as the midges that cloud the air near dungheaps, indicated that crows had found a dying animal.

A small group of men were watching a chaff-cutter and a tube-well in the shade of a mango tree. Two blindfolded bullocks pulled the stake to turn the metal cogs between which the straw was crushed, and a cart lined with jute sacking waited to carry the chaff to a nearby village where it would be stored in conical heaps and covered with a straw thatch. In a neighbouring field an old man was working a traditional plough behind a pair of bullocks, churning straight furrows in the fine alluvial soil as he walked with trance-like concentration in which time was forgotten. His long hair and beard were nearly white, his face was burned and lined by scores of years in the sun, but his old thick-veined hands still grasped the plough with strength. I thought he must be about eighty years old but Mr B said he would be nearer sixty-five: whatever his exact age he was a grand old figure and I felt diffident about photographing him.

He was happy enough though, but when I wanted a close-up shot the old man hurried away agitatedly towards the hut by the tube-well, leaving me standing nonplussed in the centre of the field. He soon returned, busily straightening his superbly unruly beard with his fingers and carrying a pair of shoes under one arm: he had not wanted to be photographed with bare feet. A younger man, a stranger to everyone in our party, then shouted out an invitation for us to eat and have tea with him, and we moved away after a polite exchange, pleading that we had to reach the nearby Radhasoami Institute.

The Radhasoami Institute on the western bank of the Beas dominates the landscape, its red mass surmounted by turrets looking like some massive confection on the yellow plain. It is the Centre for an offshoot of a sect founded by a Hindu banker from Agra in the mid-

9 Snake-charmer at Dhilwan, in the Punjab

10 Shoemaker by the Grand Trunk Road in the Punjab

11 The Nautch girl in the Dalmandi, Benares

nineteenth century. The banker's doctrine was an eclectic one, embracing something of both Hinduism and Sikhism, and when he died the movement he started split into two sub-sects, the main one remaining at Agra while a branch was started near the Beas by a Sikh disciple who was followed as guru by a succession of Sikhs.

We were shown around the grounds by a New Zealander who had travelled to India especially to stay at the Institute. He spoke reverently of the latest guru, 'the Master'. Disciples of the master were not expected to change their religion, he said. 'All we have to do is refrain from alcohol, do good and meditate for three or four hours a day.' The sect claims to have over a million followers throughout the world and the Institute is famous in the Punjab, but my companions were sceptical and admitted that this was the first time they had ever visited the place.

It was dark by the time we came back to the Grand Trunk Road on our way home. Neither cycle had a light, front or rear; a cycle with a lamp is a rarity in India. Only the pinpoint lights of stars lit the sky and the road itself was black, throwing up in our path islands that puffed like labouring cows as we sped past. We stopped when Mr Butalia somehow recognized a cyclist coming from Dhilwan—it was Mr Kunder Singh, the Family Planning Educator, with one of his subordinates, both very excited because they had heard of a Beas man who might be interested in Family Planning. Everyone thrilled as to a chase and after a brief colloquy we sped back to Beas to find the man concerned 'and show him some contraceptives'. But though we enquired among the mud-walled houses on the outskirts of Beas we never found our man. Mr Kunder Singh's information had been inaccurate. Frustration was quickly converted to energy and the cyclists raced back along the Grand Trunk Road. Mr B's cycle, with myself astern, won easily, careering over the narrow bridge past the thatched hut where the sentries sat, and breasting the other bank just ahead of an impatient lorry that had been unable to pass. The auxiliary nurse's cycle came in a poor second, having dropped a pedal en route.

Punjabis are a race of big men and they eat well. We had eaten a heavy breakfast, had lunched off parathas stuffed with meat and spices, and now at Mr Butalia's house we set to on a three-course dinner. After the meal the conversation turned to marriage. Mr Rajandass said that he had a cousin in England who had recently married a British girl against the advice of his family in the Punjab:

the marriage should not have taken place, he said, because the girl could never become part of the family, could never be like the women of the Punjab. The notion of a love marriage troubled all my companions and they were unable to conceive of the possibility of such a thing occurring in their own villages; selection for marriage on such a basis seemed to them to be blindly illogical, and they considered that the high divorce rate and homeless children in the West were a natural consequence. They all agreed however that they knew men who would have preferred bachelor freedom but had allowed their families to arrange marriages for them.

I woke early in the cool misty hour when objects in the fields seem to have swelled to three times their normal size, and waking men cough harshly as they draw their shawls around them. An early start would have been possible but for a new toaster Mr Butalia had recently bought in Delhi, which he insisted on using though the weak electric power took nearly half-an-hour to bring a faint gleam to the element and another half-hour to toast the bread.

Rucksack on back, I was finally about to leave Dhilwan, when Mr Butalia and Mr Rajandass made urgent motions for me to drop my rucksack and follow them round the Health Centre building. They walked round the building, hands behind their backs, trying rather unsuccessfully to look nonchalant, the object of their interest being a young couple standing on the steps of one of the staff quarters. They seemed an unexceptional pair, but apparently I was wrong; they had made a love marriage and everyone wanted to see them.

6

It was nearly 11.30 am before I set out for the Grand Trunk Road. A cool breeze was blowing and I could think of nothing pleasanter than the prospect of a day's walk ahead. Freedom was delicious and I felt sorry for the fellow I had seen earlier in the morning squatting in one of the cold stone cells built into each side of the gate to the police station. He had been wrapped in a thin shawl, his head sunk into his neck like an ailing bird.

Two boys accompanied me for a short way. One told me that his father was in England where he and his mother and sister hoped to join him the following year. I was now in the Jullundur Doab, that part of the Punjab lying between the Beas and Sutlej rivers, an area that has been to the fore in sending immigrants to the United Kingdom. In the days of British rule, and especially in the last century, men left their families behind in England to come to India for honour and a modest reward; now the flow had been reversed. Many a family in this area was dependent on what the breadwinner sent from abroad, and was waiting stoically for the day when they would be reunited.

The Grand Trunk Road after Dhilwan was similar to the stretch before Gujrat in Pakistan, with side ways for slow traffic and a broad macadamized central road, but the side lanes here were marshy and had obviously not been used for some years; herdsmen preferred to use the main road, and the ribs of a recently killed buffalo illustrated one of the penalties for doing so. This centre road was only just wide enough for two trucks to pass, yet herdsmen allowed their charges to straggle across the way until trucks with horns blaring were almost upon them. Bullock-cart drivers were little more careful. Their carts had no brakes, but it was explained to me that bullocks are trained to stop. Cyclists too were a menace, pedalling three abreast and I was surprised that I had seen few accidents on my way.

A young man walked with me for some miles and urged me to visit Kartarpur, a famous Sikh town lying by the Grand Trunk

Road on the way to Jullundur. Here, he said, I would find a gurdwara with a miraculous tank in which a person who suffered from pimples had only to bathe once in order to be cured. I assured him that I had no pimples. He had a lively mind but lived in a world of wonders, for though he lived and worked in nearby Kapurthala his home was in Pathankot in the north and his spirit was in the Kangra Valley with its many temples and strange beliefs. His eyes dilated with excitement when he spoke of Kangra and it was evident that his training—he said that he was a physics graduate—had done nothing to divorce wonder from reason.

Kartarpur was founded in the late sixteenth century by the Sikhs' fourth Guru, Arjun. His son, Hargobind, the fifth Guru, was the first to fire the Sikhs with the idea that they could defy the Moghuls, and Kartarpur was the site of a battle in which he defeated Moghul troops sent to arrest him. When I reached Kartarpur, after a bus ride for which the conductor would accept no payment, the first thing I wanted to see was the miraculous tank. No-one I questioned knew anything about it, though one man pointed out an advertisement painted on the town walls, which recommended some specific treatment for spots. In fact the only construction of any note in the town was the tall white gurdwara.

My neighbour on the bus to Jullundur was a middle-aged man whose jaunty manner could not disguise the tired dejection of his eyes and the resigned slump of his shoulders: he had come for a holiday to his home near Jullundur after eighteen years in England and said that even in his own village no-one knew him. Now he was staying in Jullundur with another returned exile, wondering whether he and his wife should return to Gravesend.

Jullundur is a brash manufacturing city, surrounded by one of the most fertile and prosperous districts in India, and the hotel near the centre where I took a room cost rather more than I was accustomed to paying. The manager was a Sikh, and he leapt up to shake my hand when I greeted him with 'Sat Sri Akal'. When I greeted him with the same words in the evening, however, he growled to his assistant in Punjabi that this fellow was undoubtedly willing with 'Sat Sri Akal', but they would see what my understanding was like when it came to paying the bill. They must have discussed my rucksack, which bore the marks of all its adventures over fifteen years, as well as the fact that I had myself carried it into the hotel.

'Chota Hazri' ('Bed Tea')—what luxuries one can obtain in India for a few pennies, and even at my hotel the charge for this was minimal. A breakfast of puris and vegetable curry outside the hotel cost the equivalent of just 2p, and then from the characterless streets of modern Jullundur I wandered into the old wards or 'mohallas' of the city, into narrow cobbled streets where I had to be as agile as the local dogs to escape being run down by cyclists. The buildings here were not so much houses as uneven human warrens of winding stairs and cubby holes and balconies, such an exciting jumble of stones that one could but wonder how families living in them managed to sort themselves out. The entrances were about two feet above the open drains on either side of the way, and in many instances steps of a sort had been made of broken mill-wheels. Pretty little structures with slender minarets and rickety domes came to view round each corner, their paintwork untended since Partition in 1947, but still brilliant in parts. Originally mosques, they were now being used as Sikh gurdwaras or Hindu temples.

A brisk little man in a suit of western cut made from handwoven tweed greeted me in one narrow lane, introduced himself very gravely as a manufacturer of boot polish and invited me to see his factory. It consisted of two small rooms just above the street, that in front being a storeroom and the one at the rear, just ten feet square with a hole in the roof for ventilation and light, housing the boot polish works. The chill morning air passed through my thick Norwegian pullover, yet the three boys who were the factory's labour force wore only vests and short-sleeved cotton shirts as they crouched over assorted empty boot-polish tins on the bare concrete floor. Two of the boys greased each empty tin with a black paste, and the other laid the tins out in neat rows; then while one filled three old metal kettles with liquid polish from a large drum, the third poured the polish into the tins after first heating each full kettle over an open flame. Old 'Cherry Blossom' and 'Kiwi' tins, even a 'Nugget' tin from New Zealand, and others marked with less famous brand names were now covered with a paper label 'Bhallu Boot Polish', and the manufacturing process was complete. Charles Dickens's blacking factory was never like this.

'See, see how they do it,' the proprietor urged, his eyes glowing with excitement. He was an engaging man who had been a refugee from Pakistan at Partition. The refugees who had come to Jullundur in those turbulent times had gone straight to the Muslim mohallas had, torn out the locks from the Muslim houses and settled there.

For ten years thereafter they had been government tenants, paying rent, and after that time they had been granted titles to the property. Now nearly every house in that lane pulsed with busy optimism as men worked at a diversity of small manufactures. The boot polish manufacturer, who said he had failed twice before starting on this venture, was confident that this time he would succeed. He had sales outlets for his product throughout the district, and hoped that he would soon be able to have his own tins made in Delhi; meanwhile local shopkeepers kept him supplied with empty tins. His neighbours were equally sanguine; one manufactured carpets and blankets, his looms nearly filling the room in which he worked; another made harmoniums; another had a small dairy; and so on down the lane.

In the heart of the old city was the Amam Naser Mosque, the largest mosque in Jullundur. It was the natural focal point of the old city and its emptiness made it an uneasy presence. A maulvi, a Muslim priest, had recently come to live there and I had a glimpse of his bearded face peering from an upper window onto the square which some twenty-three years earlier had been the centre of the Muslim community. The surrounding area with its winding streets, cow byres, muddy yards and tall, secretive walls was reminiscent of Gujrat in Pakistan.

Bus travel in the Punjab is cheap and convenient, with frequent services provided by the government-owned Punjab Roadways and a number of private companies. The main difference between government and private bus transport is that the former allows aboard only as many passengers as there are seats to accommodate them, whereas the latter will willingly accept all who can manage to crowd on, because the drivers and conductors receive a commission on every ticket sold. I travelled by bus from Jullundur to Phillaur on the Sutlej, once the last outpost of Ranjit Singh's empire, intending to walk from there to Ludhiana and hoping that I might find a village en route where I could stay the night.

Two Sikhs on bicycles raced by on the outskirts of Phillaur, pedalling frantically up a rise regardless of oncoming traffic and the railway crossing on the top. One skidded at the crossing and fell in the middle of the lines, blocking the road, but fortunately no traffic was passing at that moment, so he rose, dusted himself, laughed and set off again after his companion who had been waiting further down the road. Both were fashionable users of the way, for traffic on the Grand Trunk Road does not normally hesitate to overtake on ramps over railway lines, or on hills, or on corners, even when traffic is approaching from the other direction. The horn it seems is considered to have magical properties: only keep it blaring and like the trumpets before Jericho it will clear the way. Oddly enough, pedestrians always walk on the left-hand side of the road, the same side as the traffic, and seem to take a fatalistic attitude to traffic thundering behind them. The government seems to be aware of the problems and has erected a number of large road signs exhorting road users to have a care: 'Don't trust to luck. Trust to safety', 'Safety First, Luck Afterwards', 'Saving time at the expense of life is no bargain'. These signs, however, are all in English, a language few truck drivers and fewer bullock-cart drivers are likely to understand.

Across the Sutlej, the Grand Trunk Road is bordered by jungle and scrub and for some miles the people I met all had a dispirited look. Then I came to a teashop in a little clearing where half a dozen old men basked in the sun and discussed the train visible in the distance, arguing among themselves as to whether it was eleven minutes early or seven minutes late. It was a tranquil spot, and I stopped for tea.

The Grand Trunk Road is a hospitable way. Within five minutes of setting out again I was sitting in a jeep with an Indian army major who was on his way to rejoin his unit in Ambala after a spell of partridge shooting.

The major proved to be a rare companion on the Grand Trunk Road, a man who was interested in the history of the area we were travelling through. In a land where religious legend is so marvellous, history is considered unrewarding by comparison, bound as it is by reality. But the Punjab should be a schoolboy's delight, so many battles have been fought there. It transpired that the area was of special significance to the major because, though he was clean-shaven, he was a Sikh, one of a growing number of Sikhs who no longer maintain the outward attributes of the Khalsa.

'We are now in what used to be the old Moghul province of Sirhind, where there was much fighting between the Sikhs and Moghul forces during the eighteenth century. Perhaps you have heard of Sirhind?'

I admitted that the name was not very familiar.

'You must see Sirhind. I will arrange for you to stay there.'

'Are there many old buildings?' I asked.

He smiled. 'Sirhind was a city, a great city, with walls that stretched for miles. It was the seat of a Moghul governor, and like Lahore, was one of the most powerful Moghul garrisons in the whole Punjab. Today it is nothing. But you will see. There is a Moghul garden and you can stay in the pavilion there.'

As we drove along he talked about Sirhind.

The death warrant of Sirhind was signed in 1706. In that year the Sikhs, who had been involved in several skirmishes with the hill rajahs of the Punjab and with Moghul forces, were finally surrounded and Guru Gobind Singh barely managed to escape. Two of his elder sons were killed, however, and two younger sons, aged nine and seven, were captured and brought to Wazir Khan, the Moghul governor of Sirhind. He had them executed. Accounts vary as to how this was done, but the Sikhs believe that the boys were buried alive in a wall of the governor's residence.

Gobind Singh died but the cause of vengeance was soon afterwards taken up by a one time ascetic who became known as Banda 'The Slave' Singh. Banda quickly raised an army, sacked the town of Samana, home of the executioners of the Sikhs' ninth Guru, and marched on Sirhind plundering a number of towns en route. Events like this took a long time, what with training and assembling armies, and it was not until several months later that Wazir Khan marched out with his army to meet Banda's forces some ten miles out of Sirhind.

It was head-on collision or nothing in those days. Wazir Khan was killed, his forces routed. Any of his men who did not flee far into the country were killed.

Banda's forces then marched into Sirhind, and as the major put it, 'Sirhind was destroyed in detail'. Efforts were made to rebuild parts of Sirhind after that, but the town was despoiled again and again during the eighteenth century by the Sikhs.

Just how thorough a job the Sikhs did is evident immediately one reaches Sirhind. There is little to see.

'The walls stretched along that line there, and along there.' The major pointed to grass covered ridges that ran far into the distance. All in fact that can be seen today of old Sirhind are the Amkhas—a summer garden and pavilion for Moghul emperors—and a few mausolea.

Banda was to fight many more battles in the next five years, but in 1715 he was defeated by Moghul forces whose retribution was consistent with the brutality of the times. Banda and his family, together with seven hundred prisoners, were led in chains to Delhi in a grisly caravan that included 700 bullock-carts filled with the severed heads of Sikhs, and on its way the caravan passed through the remains of Sirhind. The executions of Banda and his followers in Delhi lasted for a week.

Open fields now stretch through what was once the thick of Sirhind.

The pavilion at the Amkhas has tall ceilings, and latticed windows so placed that they catch the softest of breezes. In its halcyon days its floors would have had thick carpets, flambeaux would have lighted every corner, and myriads of servants and girl companions would have breathed life into the walls.

Now it was being used as a PWD Resthouse, and the major had me installed there for the night before he continued to Ambala. The poor traveller should not complain if he is given a place where royalty has slept, but I passed an uneasy night, for the pavilion had many doors, most without bolts, small animals scampered about, and there was no lighting of any sort.

In the morning, though, I could imagine myself a monarch, as I promenaded in the formal garden in front of the pavilion, albeit the four square pools were now filled with stagnant water and the stone-work was crumbling. The garden area had once been the Diwan i Khas, the Court of Private Audience, and beyond its outer wall was a broad courtyard, the Diwan-i-Am, the Court of Public Audience, where the Emperor would meet his subjects on his occasional visits to Sirhind.

Half a mile from the Amkhas on an otherwise deserted plain, a Sikh temple marked the spot where the two elder children of Guru Gobind Singh who had been killed in Sirhind had been cremated. A mile further west another gurdwara stood over the ruins of what had been Wazir Khan's stronghold, where Sikhs believe the two other children were interred alive in the walls. In between the two gurdwaras was a small shrine on the spot where a Sikh band had harried the grisly caravan taking Sikh heads to Delhi after the capture of Banda.

'Sikh religion has been one of sacrifice', observed a tall Sikh as I passed the shrine, and in the easy manner of India he invited me to attend the betrothal ceremony of his niece, whose marriage he had arranged. A large party of the girl's relatives would be going in two tractors and trailers to the home of the boy to whom she was to be engaged, and he was expecting them at any moment.

It sounded interesting and sure enough two tractors were soon chugging towards us, the trailers laden with the relatives, some twenty men in each, with their heads just visible over the sides. I accepted the invitation, was given a place of honour on the mud-guard of one of the tractors, and soon we were in the country bumping along an extremely dusty road. Wheat, sugar-cane and mustard stretched away to the horizon promising a fine harvest. The recent introduction of Mexican variety wheat had doubled the grain yield and this together with improved winter crops of cotton and groundnuts was bringing wealth to the farmers. Traditionally farmers' houses were all in villages, but here and there isolated stone houses showed where the richer farmers had moved from their villages to live on their farms.

It seemed a long way, and when at last we came to a small settlement we appeared to have arrived. Everyone alighted from the trailers but instead of going towards the houses, spread along the road beside the fields, they squatted; this was nothing more than an easing stage along the journey, though it was difficult to understand why they chose to urinate at that spot within sight of the houses after we had been in uninhabited country for so long. This settlement was probably where my host bought the bottle he later produced from inside his coat at the betrothal ceremony.

Many traditions are now being broken in the cities of India, but in the villages they are still followed. In this case the boy and girl who were to be married had never met and would not do so until their marriage, which was planned for the following year: only the boy would be at the betrothal ceremony. The marriage had been arranged on the girl's side by her uncle, the Sikh who had invited me to the ceremony. The marriage agent on the boy's side was a Brahman health worker at his village. Much would depend on the judgement of the marriage broker as to the suitability of the girl: he would have had to investigate the antecedents and the financial standing of her family and report on her appearance.

The betrothal ceremony was held in the courtyard of a large mud-walled house and conducted by the granthi, the Sikh who had been appointed to look after the local gurdwara and to read the Granth. The Granth, the holy book of the Sikhs, was carried ceremoniously from the temple to the courtyard, a whisk being waved over it to ensure that all evil and such irritants as flies were kept away from it, for the Granth has a special sanctity for Sikhs and is regarded with a degree of reverence that one does not find in Western attitudes to the Bible. The Granth is held by Sikhs to be the symbol of Nanak and the nine gurus who followed him, the tenth guru having told his followers shortly before he died that there were to be no more gurus after him, and that henceforth Sikhs should regard the Granth as their constant guide.

The ceremony was attended only by men. The boy, who had as yet no hairs on his face, sat with senior members of his family under a canopy, while the rest of us sat in the open as the granthi chanted prayers. Then while the boy continued to look modestly at the ground, relatives of the boy's betrothed—the men whom I had accompanied from Sirhind—rose in turn and presented the lad with gifts of money, relatively small amounts, dropping the notes into a cloth he held before him.

Now it was the turn of the boy's family, and they too received gifts according to their relationship; a blanket for this man, two rupees for that, and so on. When all the presents had been given the granthi rose to distribute prasad—food that he had blessed—and all the children clamoured for their share, their hands outstretched. Prasad, a compound of sugar, flour and raisins, is at once nourishing and tasty and is given by the granthi at all Sikh services; it is a clever way of endearing the granthi to children, as well as being symbolic of the care of the church.

My difficulties of the day began after the ceremony, when my companion, he who had invited me to join the party, produced a bottle of locally made '50 per cent spirit' from somewhere inside his jacket, poured out a half glass of the neat fluid and looked to me to finish it at a draught. When I protested that I would much rather sip it, all those around me laughed.

'My dear,' said my companion heavily, 'you want to learn about Punjabis, about our life? Then you must do as we do. I must be your teacher. It is only 50 per cent and I have more here.' He patted the bulge in the breast pocket of his 'imported' tweed jacket, and I was struck by the disadvantage of visiting an isolated and delightfully rustic village when I had to rely on my companions for transport. I had intended to go to Ambala that evening but it was already mid-afternoon and no-one showed any inclination to return home. Glasses were filled and refilled. When we did leave I decided to stay at the PWD Resthouse again but it was no use trying to refuse the invitation of my host to stay at his brother's farm 'just beyond Sirhind'. It was a matter of honour he exclaimed, waving his arms, that as a foreigner I should be the guest of one of his family. When we reached Sirhind the wedding guests dispersed. A bottle of 'Black Knight', one of India's premier whiskies was purchased in the bazaar, and three of us rode on a tractor into the night, the driver being my host for the night. The farmhouse was rather isolated, half a mile from the nearest village, and there I was accommodated in a newly built guesthouse together with a trio of Sikh landowners, all idlers according to my host, but jovial ones, who to my surprise, because Sikhs are forbidden tobacco, were all heavy smokers. We dined in the family residence. My companion was morosely drunk by this time, but his brother played his part as host very punctiliously, investing me with a revolver and a heavy bandolier loaded with ammunition, as well as an overcoat of heavy blue woollen cloth, the first as a symbol of my freedom of the house, and the second, as I understood it, a signal honour conferring on me the privilege of travelling on the Northern Railway free of charge.

'No-one will ask you for the fare in the whole of the Punjab. This is the coat of an officer of the Indian Railways.' After the meal I was more sorry to hand back the coat than the revolver.

I was given a charpai in the same room as the other guests, with a cotton dhurry (mat) spread on it for a mattress, and a cotton resai (quilt) for covering. Trains between Amritsar and Sirhind passed within twenty-five yards of my head, a badly-tuned radio was turned on at full volume, and the neon light was left on all night, yet once I was curled under my resai I slept within minutes. Next morning after a breakfast of parathas, pure white butter and spinach cooked in oil, I set off for the Grand Trunk Road delighted that I was once more in command of my day, and happy to leave blighted Sirhind.

A horn blared, dust mushroomed and a bus drew up before me, the conductor leaning from the doorway to beckon me aboard. He would accept no payment, and a middle-aged Sikh inspector for the bus company suggested that I alight at his village and be his guest 'for a week or so, for as long as you wish'. I declined the kind offer, but he would not let me part from him till I had eaten lunch with him at Rajpura, at one of the eating shops around the bus station square under the great walls of a serai built by the Moghuls.

The sole of my right shoe had begun to flap and sent up little clouds of dust on the road past Rajpura. This stretch of the way followed the alignment of Sher Shah Suri's road and a couple of kos minars were still in fair condition, bare sloping pillars of bricks and mortar, some twenty feet high and rounded at the top, which had been set along the road to mark the stages and also the way itself in Sher Shah Suri's time when all this land had been jungle. As I plodded along, fit enough by this stage to enjoy the freedom of the road rather than being conscious all the time of the weight of my rucksack, a motor cycle pulled up ahead of me and the rider divested himself of helmet and goggles.

'Hullo old man, going far? Can I give you a lift to Ambala?'

'Well, no thanks. I had a lift a short way back, and I'm just plodding on for a while enjoying the countryside.'

'Good show. Come and see me when you reach Ambala. I'm with Hodson's Horse, on a posting to Ambala cantonment. You'll find me at the Deccan Horse.'

He was young and exuberant, and looked at his dusty machine with pride. Hodson's Horse is perhaps the most famous cavalry regiment in India.

'I've no other clothes than these I stand in,' I said, thinking it unlikely that I would be welcome beyond the guardhouse at the Deccan Horse.

'Never mind,' he roared as he started his machine again. 'We'll fix you up with clothes and give you a hot bath too. Expect you soon.' And he was off, trailing a growing parachute of dust.

Three flyblown food-stalls, a railway station and an old Moghul serai constituted Shambhu, a settlement six miles beyond Rajpura along the Grand Trunk Road. The whole population lived in the serai. Two bitches skulked between the benches at one of the food-stalls, their eyes like slits in their sharp heads, their backbones keen as blades between stiff necks and fleshless haunches, animals of a nightmare with their long thin tails low and inert. If their tails ever did rise, it would probably be with the stiffness that is the mark of rabies and then the men would kill them with their sticks. Until such time, they would be allowed to live, belonging to no-one, all but lifeless yet still able to give birth to puppies and to feed them for a while from flaccid teats. Two puppies lay in the yard, eyes half closed with some purulent excretion. A third puppy was more fortunate and appeared to have been adopted by a fruit vendor who sat in the dust by the Grand Trunk Road with a few guavas before him on a cloth and occasionally gave the puppy a piece of fruit.

Shambhu serai lay in the midst of wheatfields, its thick brown walls enclosing a courtyard of some four acres. Recesses with sunken floors in the outer walls were once rooms for wayfarers and now the permanent home of families working on the surrounding land. A sprucely-dressed Sikh appeared from one of the recesses and invited me to tea, and joining him I found myself in a tidy, whitewashed room with an arched ceiling where four young women sat knitting demurely round a table laid for tea. They were all teachers at Shambhu Primary School in the old serai, and travelled there each day from their homes in Ambala, thirteen miles away. They were not interested in this romantic schoolhouse; it was merely inconveniently remote and as to its age, modernity would have excited them more.

I travelled with them in a bus to Ambala, and was about to leave the bus station there when I noticed that one of the bus indicators showed CHANDIGARH. As Chandigarh is within walking distance of Kasauli, where I was born, and of Sanawar, where I spent the greater part of my first fifteen years, I changed my immediate plans and joined the bus queue.

7

A long queue of passengers was waiting for the Chandigarh bus outside the shaky wooden shack that served for a ticket office at Ambala City bus station. Very remarkably it was an orderly queue. When the queue behind me was almost as long as that in front, an old man pointed to an empty bus that had been standing in the yard all the time that I had been there and shouted: 'Get on board. There are seats for all. You can buy your tickets on the bus.'

Wise by now to the technique of travelling in India, I was first aboard and claimed a front seat. The orderly queue broke and everyone surged towards the two bus doors, women carrying babies battling with the rest. When the loose scrum inside the bus sorted itself out at last and the full load of passengers was settled and in good humour, a beggar clambered aboard and wailed for alms.

'What's this? The government taxes us and now you have come,' shouted a passenger and everyone laughed. The beggar alighted and collected a number of small coins handed down by passengers from the windows. Then we were off on the Kalka road, a handsome tree-lined way, the main road to the hill station, Simla, which in British days was the summer capital of India. Chandigarh is ten miles before Kalka, thirty from Ambala, and we reached it in the late afternoon.

The capital of the undivided Punjab before Independence Day had been Lahore. After Partition, Lahore remained the capital of West Punjab in Pakistan, but the East Punjab, the Indian portion of the State, was left without a capital, and so Chandigarh was built to fill the need after international architects, including Le Corbusier and Maxwell Fry, had been called in to design it. The result is still rather startling.

It seems on first acquaintance to be the sort of city that might be built on a sea-bed, a science fiction city, a strange world for warm, gregarious Punjabis. Its long concrete rows stretch across the dusty Kalka plain towards the welcome irregularity of the Kasauli Ridge to the north, but the geometrical patterns have not altogether stifled the native talent for warm disorder: rows of bazaar tents and flimsy shacks, the stands of cobblers and peanut vendors under banyan and neem trees, and other makeshift shelters break the severity of the lines. It is still a raw city, but both man and Nature are establishing themselves and one day it will take its place among the most gracious cities on the subcontinent.

That night, a wedding procession passed through the centre of Chandigarh, right by the little guesthouse where I had a room, deriding the still modernity of Chandigarh with the uninhibited noise that only an Indian country band can make, the musicians being paid not so much, one would judge, for their musical ears and ability as for their stamina. Heading the procession was a clarinettist, a man of great wind who set the fast pace and maintained it, sometimes solo when the drums and bugles sank briefly into silence. Behind him were buglers, and then came the bridegroom on a gorgeously caparisoned horse, as richly decorated as his mount, peering from behind the golden tassels that hung about his face. Other members of the band followed, the percussion squad, and behind them was the main body of the guests, friends and relatives of the bridegroom going to the house of the bride-to-be, where the wedding ceremony would be held. Scattered among the band and followers were the lamp bearers, supporting on their shoulders the brilliant paraffin lamps that in the intense darkness of the Indian night burnished the fairy gold of the bridegroom's equipage, and exaggerated the extravagant colours of the bandsmen's uniforms. The guests, though more soberly dressed, were in spirited mood: after every hundred yards or so the procession stopped, the bandsmen deployed themselves facing the procession, leaving a space between themselves and the bridegroom, and into this clearing pranced the more animated guests, coats unbuttoned, hair awry, to leap and sway in an extemporized version of the Bhangra, the famous Punjabi country dance, a dance that has its origins in the graceful motions of women winnowing corn in the fields.

In the bad old days in India, when the village money-lenders held the countryfolk in thrall, a major cause of indebtedness was prodigal expenditure on weddings, because a man's honour depended on a fine show. Now, with the spread of education, people are less extravagant in many ways, but—especially in the Punjab—they still have no inclination to economize on their wedding celebrations. I was assured that this particular celebration was a very ordinary affair, but it seemed as exciting as the Big Top, and I joined in the procession at the rear, following it for about three-quarters of a mile before returning to my quarters.

'Pear-purrr . . . Pear-purrr Maharaj.' The cries of the newspaper-seller constituted reveille next morning. Chandigarh looked more attractive in the early morning, when the sun had not yet had time to sharpen the concrete corners of the buildings. The early morning breeze was cool, the sky a clear, light blue, and for a moment as I stood in the modern street I could fancy myself somewhere in northern Scandinavia, until rickshaw boys strained past, standing on their pedals. The Kasauli Ridge stood out clear to the north; the sharp slope of Monkey Point, the Upper Ridge, and the slope down to the lower bazaar. It would be very pleasant to walk up there by the nine-mile short-cut from Kalka, certainly preferable to hurrying south to Patiala on the afternoon bus.

Between Chandigarh and Kalka lies the showpiece of the Hariana State Tourist Board, the Moghul garden at Pinjore, and the buses going there were filled with families from Chandigarh setting out for a Sunday afternoon picnic. A quartet of old women begged under great eucalyptus trees along the approach to the garden entrance, and an old strident-voiced man bellowed for alms to feed himself and his fat drowsy python, which was wound about his neck and shoulders.

The garden was built for the Emperor Aurangzeb by the man responsible for the Badshahi Mosque in Lahore, Fadai Khan, and those being troublous times it was surrounded by a stout wall. When Moghul power declined the garden was neglected and, according to a Tourist Board pamphlet, 'the striped and ferocious tigers of Pinjore made the lovely garden their haunt'. It later became the property of the Maharajah of Patiala, and the garden and Moghul summerhouses were restored. Now it is a very pretty place, with the garden dropping in a series of terraces, water cascading down a central channel past little groves of mangoes and other fruit trees, clusters of bougainvillaea and rows of sweetpeas.

A surprising and enchanting feature of the scene was a bevy of seven girls who were dancing and singing on the lawn and boldly answering quips made by soldiers from a large tent encampment nearby. They were out for the day from college in Chandigarh and they, more than the new city, symbolized progress in India. They had as many incentives as had those who were of their age at Independence, together with a better sense of direction and more confidence. Shades of the past emperors! The sprightly girls discovered a bearded young Swede sitting on his rucksack in a corner of the garden and, gazing uninhibitedly into his blue eyes, they insisted that he join them for lunch. And then they discovered me, but I could offer no competition to Gert, the Swede, with his blue eyes.

Gert was a hitch-hiker on his way from Sweden to Australia and he had come to Pinjore to have a glimpse of the Hills. I suggested he walk with me to Kasauli, about 4,200 feet above us, at an altitude of 6,300 feet, and he agreed. The girls gave us a lift to the foot of the nine-mile short-cut at Kalka and we were soon looking down on a goods train crawling round the bends of the Kalka-Simla narrow gauge railway track. A camel padded down the path towards us laden with firewood, and it seemed an appropriate animal for the dry hillside dotted with cacti.

Higher up, the hillside had been terraced and planted with wheat, and at times the vertical distance between the narrow terraces was greater than their width. The flat-roofed mud houses of the little villages still contrived to keep cattle and goats, and had more than enough dung for making fuel. One short-cut through a village that would have had a superb view over the plains and the river Sutlej on a fine day, necessitated the traverse of a pungent dungheap and an upward scramble along the edge of a landslide. I was delighted to see that Gert, who had mentioned that he was a keen walker and had started with a brisk stride, was now allowing me to set the pace; I had not disclosed to him that these were my hills, Kasauli my birthplace and that Sanawar on a neighbouring ridge had been my home for nearly fifteen years.

We reached Kasauli's lower bazaar three hours after starting from Kalka, which must be par on that track for men with rucksacks, and hurried into the first tea shop. This was built in the characteristic Kasauli bazaar style from flattened petrol tins and cans that had once contained cooking fat, fastened to a wooden framework. The building materials had been thrown out from the British military cantonment in Kasauli before Independence, and had been repaired with materials thrown out by the Indian troops who had succeeded the British, but however humble the exterior, the interior was snug and comfortable, with wrought-iron chairs ranged around a long table under a sloping roof. When I was a boy one could only have tea at the Alasia or the Maurice Hotel in Kasauli and the bazaar had been considered filthy, but now, perhaps because of my simple life on the road, the bazaar appeared clean, and was certainly free of the scarlet discolorations that had in British days occasioned the public notice 'Expectoration forbidden'.

Gert said that during the month he had been in India he had never paid for his accommodation, having slept in private houses and on railway stations, but I felt I was too near home to sleep rough, and we shared a room at the Maurice Hotel.

This is one of the ramshackle wooden structures full of balconies and eaves and topped with a roof of corrugated iron, which is common in the Simla Hills. Prior to 1947 it had been a fairly popular resort hotel, but now it was a mausoleum for memories, creaky, draughty and barely furnished. It was, however, cheap and therefore what we wanted. Having settled for a room, or rather a suite with a lounge, bedroom, and bathroom, all containing the sad cracked and dusty furniture of a quarter of a century and more ago, we were just in time to see the last light on the Sanawar Ridge, the next ridge to the north, where the sun's rays spotlighted the red tin roofs and the pine trees. Beyond Sanawar the great bowl in the hills, with Sabathu at its centre, was in shadow and beyond that the high snow peaks were grey.

I was tempted to walk across to Sanawar but decided not to do so, for home as it had been to me, it still is a school and I did not feel that the pupils would be edified by my appearance at this time. Had I gone there on this occasion it would have been my second visit in recent years: my first visit there as an old boy had been made two years previously, and had been a happy one.

One memory of Sanawar that I had carried away with me when my family left India in 1950 was of highly polished boots and belts and buckles and buttons and badges, but the dominant memories had been of slopes covered with pine-needles and the beauty of the surrounding hills; the Kasauli Ridge to the south and in the north the great forest bowl that rises to Simla and is bordered on the horizon by snows of the higher Himalayas.

The world had not passed through Sanawar, nor come to its door. Sanawar had been an isolated community; a boarding school which, apart from receiving regular supplies from Kasauli, three miles away, was almost self-sufficient. The Sanawar of my day had its own dairy, hospital, printing works, Public Works Department office, electric plant, carpenters' and plumbers' workshops and it had rarely been necessary to call in outside help for any jobs that needed doing. Sanawar had been an inward-looking community: the staff had their own club and did not often leave the school, and children stayed at the school for ten months of the year, with very infrequent visits to the Kasauli cinema. Single staff rarely brought in outsiders when they married, and most of the staff in my time seemed to have lived on the hilltop for decades.

The school had been founded in 1847, at a time when British rule was first being introduced to the Punjab, and was named after its founder, Sir Henry Lawrence, then British Resident at Lahore, who having served in India for more than twenty years had seen enough of barrack life in the plains to realize the need for a school where the children of British troops could be sent for their education away from the heat of the plains. The success he achieved through his campaigning for the school can be seen in the list of donations and subscriptions received in the first ten years of Sanawar's life, when everybody who was somebody in India appears to have made a contribution.

The Sanawar Ridge, named after a village at its foot, was chosen because it combined 'most of the requisites for any asylum, viz: isolation, with ample space and plenty of water, at a good height in a healthy locality'. Construction of the school's first buildings was supervised by Lieutenant William Hodson, who was to become famous as Hodson of Hodson's Horse.

'I have the sole direction and control of nearly four hundred and fifty workers', Hodson wrote at the time, 'including paying them, keeping accounts, drawing plans and everything. I have to get the earth dug for the bricks, see the moulds made, and watch the progress of them till the kiln is full, get wood for the kiln and direct the lighting of the same, and finally provide a goat to sacrifice to the demon who is supposed to turn the bricks red!'

The school was officially opened in March 1847 by Mrs George Lawrence, Sir Henry's sister-in-law, whose husband, then in Peshawar, was one of the famous band of administrators along the North West Frontier. With such beginnings Sanawar could not but become a pinker shade of pink on the broadening flush of the British Empire.

One of the first concerns of the school was with cleanliness. 'In all large institutions of a similar character to this in England, it is found most important, as conducive to health and preventive to skin diseases, that the children should be bathed in summer at least twice or thrice in the week in slightly tepid water; cold water bathing I found not to agree with children of a SCROFULOUS tendency and this tendency is the more common in the class we have to do with.' So wrote the school's first Principal in one of his earliest reports to the School Committee. 'The class we have to do with' were, as the founder had intended, the orphans and other children of British private soldiers and non-commissioned officers serving in India. Fees were graded according to circumstances: privates and corporals for example could send their children to Sanawar without paying any fee and the fee charged to sergeants major, holders of the highest rank among parents, was nominal.

A military form of organization was introduced in the school, and an early report states that 'the children were paraded to the sound of the bugle, and were taught the duty of prompt obedience by being made to go through their various duties with military precision'. They were awakened each morning between five and six o'clock, and were filed off to the lavatory after a moment for private prayer. After washing and dressing they were inspected, and were then free 'for recreation'—a very loose term, which from my own experience at Sanawar ninety years or so later probably meant cleaning jobs of some kind—until breakfast at 7.30 am. Morning prayer was at 9 am and when that was over the children were marched to their classrooms for the first class session. A half-hour of recreation followed the end of morning school and then 'orderly-room' was held, a time of inquisition and punishment of misdemeanours, the usual punishments being detention or strokes on the hand; if, however, some major offence had been committed, such as 'stealing or indecency', the wrong-doer was flogged by one of the school sergeants in the presence of the Principal at a special parade of all the boys. Dinner at 1 pm was followed by afternoon school between 2 pm and 4 pm and this was concluded with evening prayers. Supper was at 5 pm and before long, at some time between 7 pm and 8 pm depending on the season, the bugle was sounding 'Lights Out'.

All this was designed for the making of the British soldier in India; in time Sanawar became a natural recruiting ground for the Army, though Sir Henry Lawrence had insisted that boys should not be allowed to enlist before the age of sixteen, when they might be presumed to know their own minds.

Sanawar was already well established by the time India came under the British Raj, and the school had evidently achieved a sort of fame by Kipling's day. When Kim finds his 'Red Bull on a green field' at last, and is taken rather against his will into the care of the Mavericks, he is told that he is to be sent to a place called Sanawar: 'You'll live to be grateful to your friend the Red Bull yet', says Father Victor. 'We'll make a man of you at Sanawar—even at the price of making you a Protestant.' But we miss a description of Sanawar in Rudyard Kipling's day, because Kim is sent to St Xavier's in Lucknow instead.

I was born at the British Military Hospital in Kasauli and then lived in Sanawar, where my father was a member of the teaching staff. I became a boarder in the Preparatory School when I was six, at which time the Lawrence Royal Military School, Sanawar, was still very much the sort of institution that its founder had envisaged. The school strength was then 530 pupils, between the ages of five and eighteen, nearly all orphans and other children of British troops who had served or were serving in India.

In the preparatory school we were spared much of the military atmosphere of the senior school, and once we had left the classroom we had splendid natural playgrounds, for the forested hillside came to the very edge of the flagged yard bordering our dormitory, from where one could glimpse between the trees the far range beyond Simla and beyond that the snows of the Himalayas. We would scramble on the hillsides; climb the pine trees almost as agilely as the regiments of red-rumped brown monkeys that seemed ever on the move in the trees and over Sanawar's corrugated iron roofs; swing on the creepers; chase butterflies, and run free about the roads. The roads were safe, for, except for the regular supply truck from Kasauli, motors rarely entered the school gate, and as to any other machines, there was no point in having a bicycle or tricycle among the hills. Sanawar did have a fire engine, but that had to be pushed by hand.

In time I graduated to the senior school and learned what makes a good soldier. The school motto was 'Never give in' but it might well have been the old stricture, 'Fear God, Honour the Queen, Shoot Straight and Keep Clean', except that we now had a King on the throne . . . When the school had been founded it had been organized on military lines, but the curriculum had been aimed at training boys for various departments in government service. Now the military system was just as rigid, the boys were 'offered opportunities of joining the armed forces' and, as the school rules had it, 'the atmosphere of the school tends towards this end'.

Our class teachers were civilians and in class one could forget that one wore uniform, but when schoolwork was over we came under the immediate control of the school's military arm—a company sergeant major who was chief instructor, a sergeant bandmaster, and a sergeant gymnastics instructor, and for these staff Sanawar seemed to have the pick of the British Army. The CSM was usually an ex-heavyweight Army Boxing Champion or Champion Sword Swinger or someone of that calibre, and the gym sergeant would be another man of extraordinary strength and agility, and neither was the sort of person a boy would think of disobeying. These military men were supposed to be under the authority of the civilian administrative staff, led by the Principal, but it seemed to us that the military had absolute power.

As in the days of nearly a hundred years before, the day was punctuated by the sound of the bugle: one woke to a piercing reveille, washed, rushed down to the latrines and rushed out again (it was too cold to linger in those concrete hutches on the hillside, for they were open in front and had a wire gauze gate at the back that the sweeper lifted to remove the can), stripped one's bed, folded one's bedclothes and made a neat pile of all one's possessions on one's bed—everything had to be folded just so many centimetres across, and so many centimetres deep. Then the bugle would call; it was time for morning drill. The bugle again for the breakfast call. After breakfast it was time to change into full uniform: boots and hose-stops and puttees, broad leather belts with large brass buckles, side caps with brass buttons, or Gurkha hats with a large brass Sanawar badge, all the leather and brass kept in shining condition. Depending on the season one wore either khaki shirt and shorts or battledress. The bugle called again: time to parade for morning chapel, and after chapel to march past the cenotaph to the long classroom block. That was the start of the day, and whenever we were away for any length of time from the classrooms, the ever-ready bugle seemed to be nearby to maintain the military tempo.

Official parades were a regular feature of the year. Whenever one of the school's official visitors, that is the Viceroy or the Governor of the Punjab, or one of the school's Board of Governors, came to Sanawar we had a full ceremonial parade. The school always put on a good show on these occasions, and certainly failure to have done so would not have been for want of practice. Sanawar had a long military tradition to maintain: it had received its first colours in 1853 from Lord Dalhousie, the then Governor General of India. The older boys carried .303 rifles with fixed bayonets on parade, and I had always aspired to do so, but it was my misfortune that Indian Independence came before I graduated from an imitation rifle with a wooden bayonet to the real thing.

Girls comprised half the school's pupils, but we saw little of them as they attended separate classes: nevertheless, romance was an important factor in school life. Boys courted girls by a system known as 'squaring'; the courtship started with a formal proposal usually sent via an intermediary, saying simply 'Will you square me?' If the girl agreed, the 'squarers' would meet under the arches on the verandah of Big School—the main classroom block—during the morning and afternoon breaks, and were sometimes able to sit together when watching major school events. Passion was frequently aroused but rarely, as far as I knew, had any opportunity of being satisfied, for boys and girls were quartered at opposite ends of the school, and at night the school chowkidars, with their spears and lanterns and rasping coughs, kept a watch not so much to prevent outsiders from entering the school area as to ensure that the two sexes had no opportunity of meeting.

This might all sound rather rugged; certainly Sanawar turned out many good soldiers and, I am sure, good soldiers' wives. Interspersed with the military regimen however were glorious free periods for butterfly hunting in summer, and pine-cone collecting over the surrounding area in the winter, and throughout the year we had the run of the ridge. The scenery, always beautiful, was sometimes spectacular, especially during the dry periods before the monsoon, when Sanawar might be ringed with forest fires, or during the monsoon when the lightning in the valleys was the Himalayan answer to the Aurora Borealis.

The centenary of the Lawrence Royal Military School, in 1947, was followed a few weeks later by Independence. British troops and their families started on their way to the UK and other stations abroad. When the school broke up for the Christmas holidays that year, most of the children were taken to the plains in a convoy of trucks with a Gurkha escort—those being troublous times in the north—and that winter Sanawar was guarded by a detachment of men from an Assamase regiment. The school's raison d'être of a hundred years no longer seemed to exist. In the next two years Sanawar started to adapt to a new rôle as a Public School, with a few dozen Indian pupils from wealthy families and a few children who remained from the previous year—most of us children of members of staff. The atmosphere at the school was now much more relaxed than formerly, but Sanawar felt empty, a sounding box echoing what had gone. However when my family left Sanawar and India in 1950 it seemed to me that we were going into exile, not in any way going home.

Some eighteen years later, two years prior to my visit to Kasauli with Gert, I climbed the bridle-path to Sanawar from Dharampore, the nearest station on the Kalka-Simla railway. I passed a man loading a mule with gravel, and met two children from the small school in Sanawar for children from nearby villages. They were walking down to Dharampore with their wooden slates in cotton bags on their backs and looked surprised to see me, as well they might, a man with a rucksack striding up the hill as if on a steeple-chase. It was quiet and the pines smelt very sweet. I passed the school cemetery, on a spur, the graves on terraces beneath the pines: I think the last time a child was buried there was in 1941 or 1942, having died from diphtheria. After that everything fitted into contours which seemed to have been photographed on my memory: every little path had its association. It was a warm, drowsy day and as I walked into Sanawar I could well have been in a dream, for there it all was, exactly as I had left it, save for an addition to the prep school dormitories, a new flight of steps or two, a railing, and a few fresh coats of paint. I could have walked blindfolded over the familiar slopes, half-drunk with old familiar scents. When I was welcomed by a member of the staff from pre-1947 days—Mr Trevor Kemp, who had been my science teacher and was now senior master—I might well have thought that I had just woken from a long sleep, and this was especially so when the Kemps invited me to stay with them and I found myself in the house that had been my home before my family left India, and had many years before that been the home of my grandparents.

I was much too excited to pay as much attention to curriculum, drama classes and school recreation as the Kemps might have wished: I could have spent weeks searching out favourite corners of old. Nevertheless, I could see that Sanawar was not a new school using old buildings: it had taken over the tradition of the past and adapted the old military organization so that though it was now less obviously military, it still retained much of the old discipline and snap. I was not at all surprised to learn that the PT instructor had held the Heavyweight boxing title in the Indian Army for several years. The school motto had been retained, so had the old school song, and a short non-denominational prayer session was held each day in the school chapel. The names of the school houses had been changed, but the names of topographical features and of school events had been retained. Sanawar's equivalent of the marathon was still the Hodson Run, and children still ran up Sergeant Tilley's Hill.

One very great change, however, was the difference between the catering in my time, and what I now saw. It is doubtful whether there had been much difference in the catering during the school's first hundred years: the regimen for the 1840s had been a daily allowance of eight ounces of meat, sixteen ounces of bread, eight ounces of rice and vegetables, sixteen ounces of milk, a quarter-ounce of sugar and 'puddings extra twice a week'. In my early days as a boarder the ration had been similar except that, as I remember, we had rather less meat but more vegetables, plus porridge and a daily portion of cheese, treacle, and the occasional egg. Now I could scarcely credit my eyes as I saw boys getting second helpings of egg curry, as many chuppattis as they could eat, fresh fruit, creamy milk, butter . . . 'They're growing boys,' was the fond remark of the lady in charge of the school catering, 'certainly they should eat as much as they want.'

A chaplain of Kasauli, visiting Sanawar in 1852 had praised various aspects of the institution's life and added: 'My only regret is that there is not another institution, conducted on precisely the same principles for the higher classes, as I feel satisfied that there are many parents who would be thankful to avail themselves of it for the Education of the Children'.

The Sanawar I had returned to appeared to be what the Chaplain had envisaged for the second institution.

8

Satisfaction at being among the hills again, and a strong vein of reminiscence, would have kept me happy that evening in Kasauli after the walk up from Kalka with Gert.

My companion, however, was more concerned with the need for a meal: he had refused to eat anything in Kasauli bazaar on our arrival for fear of disease and was therefore the more disappointed when our hotel held out little hope of supper. We had come before the tourist season and the hotel did not hold stocks of food. Eventually food was found and, as is the style in more famous restaurants, we were shown the ingredients of our meal before they were cooked, the three wrinkled carrots and the nobbly potatoes being held up in what looked like a laundry basket for inspection: these would provide the material for a 'vegetable curry' and rice would supply the bulk. Then a fire was started in the cavernous kitchen and smoke slowly filled the neighbouring dining room where we were waiting, as efforts were made to get a blaze from damp wood. During the hour that we waited Gert solved his problems by going into a trance. Then the meal arrived, a great heap of rice and a bowl of potato curry; the three carrots had disappeared without trace. Gert cleared two soup-bowls of rice and declared at the end that he had not eaten a better meal in India.

That over, Gert retired to our room, stretched out on the only sound bed of the two, and was soon asleep, leaving me to cope with the creaky wooden frame with sagging grey tape supports that was my own bed for the night; I had no doubt whatever that Gert would succeed in hitch-hiking to Australia as he planned.

The haze that had obscured the view of the plains on our way up from Kalka persisted next morning, but the mountains beyond Simla, the sentinels of Central Asia, were clear. Gert decided that he had already spent long enough in the hills. I would have been happy to stay in the area for a much longer period and decided to make a short visit to Simla, so when Gert opted to travel by the bus to Kalka

I went with him as far as Dharampore, a station on the Kalka-Simla Railway.

The approach to Simla by the Kalka-Simla Railway is one of the delights of a visit to the hill station. The train climbs some 4,800 feet on its sixty-mile journey from Kalka and the route is a serpentine one even though as many corners are cut as possible, with 103 tunnels on the way. The Mail train takes six hours and 37 minutes for the run, time enough for the traveller to get an idea of the extent of the hills and to be freshened by the delicious scent of the pines long before he reaches his destination.

Wherever one looks from the train one sees pine forests stretching over the slopes, and the scent of the pines reminded me of boyhood picnics in summer and of pine-cone hunts in the winter when we gathered great sacksful of the handsome cones. The pines (pinus longifolia) are sturdy and beautiful, with large open cones, sprigs of light green needles, and thick flaky bark that is ideal material for making toy boats, or for schoolboy engravings of hearts and arrows and other tokens of love; their trunks are thick and strong, their branches stout and well-spaced for climbing; their needles can be plaited into chains; their cones burn easily with a crackling roar, and the little nuts hidden in the cones are crisp and tasty. The pines are part of the soul of the Simla Hills.

The Simla terminus of the Kalka-Simla Railway is near the lower bazaar, that 'crowded rabbit-warren that climbs up from the valley to the Town Hall at an angle of forty-five', as Kipling described it, and coming to the bazaar I asked an elderly Sikh shopkeeper for advice on where I should stay.

'Have a care, have a care', he roared. 'I must tell you that the hotel people here are looters, LOOTERS. If you do stay at a hotel, do not eat there, for some hotels make a seemingly moderate charge for a room and overcharge for meals.'

He advised me to stay at a nearby dharamsala (the word means 'religious abode'), an inn of a sort that is a feature of nearly every city and town in India. Dharamsalas are run on a non-profit-making basis, and are usually built by rich traders, either as an act of genuine philanthropy, or as a means of perpetuating their names. They are a great boon to modest travellers as they rarely charge more than one rupee per night per person for a bed.

The recommended dharamsala was a freshly-painted, concrete building anchored somehow to the steep slope about a hundred feet below the Mall, and surrounded by rusty metal structures, sheds and shops, temples and cheap hotels, which appeared to be perched one on top of the other in a tangle that no architect would conceive to be possible. Long flights of steps and steep narrow paths led to the Mall, and heavily burdened coolies moved slowly on the slopes, veins bulging in their necks as they took the weight of their loads by a strap which passed round the forehead. There was room at the dharamsala, and I was free to explore.

'Simla is celebrated as a retreat for those seeking renovation of health or relief from the oppressive heat of the plains of Hindustan,' states the 1854 edition of the Gazeteer of the East India Company. At this time the houses of Simla were scattered irregularly over the Ridge, and the only way of reaching the hill station from the plains was by pony or jampan (a sedan chair with curtains). Two years after that a road to Simla was completed, and travel to the hills was by tonga and ekka (a pony-trap of a more primitive type than a tonga). The Kalka-Simla Railway was opened in 1903, by which time Simla's fame was already well established, as it had been the summer capital of India since 1865.

I spent two winters in Simla as a boy, and was lucky to be there during the winter of 1944/5, when the settlement received its heaviest snowfall of the century. Nearly eight feet of snow was recorded that winter and, as I was able to buy a fine toboggan for just two rupees and as the roads that ran down from the Mall made perfect toboggan runs, Simla that winter was paradise.

Now, on my return to the 'Queen of the Hills', I found Simla to be as lively as I remembered it, possibly more so, because I could now wander at will in the lower and the Lakkar bazaars, areas I had seldom entered as a boy. Simla's major glories, its peerless situation and the beauty of the forested ridge and the deodar-covered Jakko Peak—these had not diminished. Many famous institutions of the fashionable Simla of British days were now closed, or were no longer to be found: the Gaiety Theatre was no longer open to the public, Annandale racecourse was reserved for military use, and Wengers, the restaurant company, had disappeared (though a branch of the firm still operates in New Delhi), but these had not been part of a boy's world when I knew them, and I did not miss them now.

I climbed Jakko, which rises some 800 feet above the Ridge. The temple of Hanuman, the Monkey God, which stands at the summit, was deserted, though a number of monkeys playing in the trees periodically touched wires that were stretched between the trees and the temple and thereby set the temple bells ringing. It was eerie up there, a chill wind was blowing, and as dusk approached the dark deodars seemed very sinister. I suddenly felt very lonely and hurried down towards the evening lights that now studded the Ridge.

A few rickshaws were still about, ancient contraptions which had a look of faded glory, as if they might once have belonged to a maharajah, and the stocky little rickshaw men were prepared to pull them up the steepest inclines, their heads down, rickshaw poles pointing to the sky. It was not yet the summer season however, and there was scant hope of custom.

Late in the evening, when the Ridge and the Mall were already asleep, life still pulsed strongly in the lower bazaar: shops were active, eating-houses full, knots of men waited hopefully in the narrow streets for something interesting to happen, and the occasional cow nosed hopefully through heaps of the day's refuse. A marriage party with an enthusiastic band of buglers and drummers in attendance was moving somewhere in the bowels of the bazaar. The occupants of the dharamsala were settling for the night when I returned, and a grey-haired gentleman was already tucked up in a bedding roll on a charpai in the double room where I had been allocated a bed. He was reading a long manuscript and scarcely glanced up when I entered. I looked dubiously at the cotton tapes on my bed, which were grey with dirt, at the feeble electric light and the broken window panes, but I knew that I was lucky to have a place to rest in, let alone some degree of privacy and electric light as well, for just one rupee. However, I am rarely as resolute in the evening as I might be at dawn.

'I wonder if there are any bed bugs?' I said, prodding the bed.

'Of course there will be,' the worthy replied, with an assurance that was horrifying.

'What can I do about them?'

'There is nothing to be done: the people who run the dharamsala will not "Flit" the rooms and the beds because it is against their belief to take any life.'

'Where do the bed bugs hide?'

'They hide in the joints of the bed and when it is dark and they feel the warmth from your body they come out.' He chuckled. 'They need food and they suck your blood: you must make a contribution.'

We decided to leave the light on to deter the bugs, but someone must have reached through a broken pane in our window, and switched off the light during the night. I had smeared myself with insect repellent before retiring, and only itched round the small of the back when I awoke next morning, but was unable to discover how my companion had fared for he had already departed when I awoke.

A traveller who comes only as far as Simla may not notice much difference between the people of the plains and the people he meets in the Simla Hills, but beyond Simla one soon meets the true paharis—the hill people. Making a day's excursion beyond Simla I travelled by bus to Narkanda, thirty-nine miles beyond Simla and at an altitude of 9,600 feet. Rain had fallen in the morning and the air was chill. My companions on the bus were hillmen, dressed in close-fitting coats, matching trousers and flat caps, all of homespun woollen material. The usual colour of the fabric was light brown, but the front of the cap was always decorated with a band of bright velvet, usually red, green or blue. One of the men, however, had a gorgeous waistcoat of green and orange homespun, which I no sooner saw than I coveted and I could scarcely take my eyes off it. I was assured that I would be able to obtain similar material in the lower bazaar in Simla, but I never saw anything as fine again.

The view from Narkanda was superb, with the main Himalayan chain clearly visible to the north-east, a wall of spiring snow peaks. The prospect of trekking into the hills was an alluring one, for it would be possible to travel by bus along the Hindustan-Tibet Road as far as Rampur, seventy-two miles from Simla, and then trek for two or three days, across the 10,750-foot high Bashleo Pass, down to Banjar and thence into the Kulu Valley, the Valley of the Gods, noted for its beautiful women, fine scenery and its excellent apples.

Early in May would be the right time for trekking, and that was when I expected to reach Calcutta at the end of the Grand Trunk Road. It would be worth returning to these hills for a week or so in May, because that would be the time of the hill melas (fairs) when the sound of drums would reverberate through the hills and the hill-folk would blow the great beaten-silver horns that each village in the region possesses, and in each village the local god would be carried on a palanquin from the temple to watch the festivities. I had been to a number of melas in the Kulu region on a previous visit to India, but on that occasion I had travelled to Kulu by bus from Chandigarh.

That night, my second in Simla, I had the room in the dharamsala to myself. The following morning, itching rather more than I had the morning before, I travelled by early bus to Kalka and thence to Ambala and arrived in the late afternoon at Ambala Cantonment, where I planned to visit the army lieutenant who had offered me a lift into Ambala on his motor cycle some days previously.

9

'Babujee u-u-uhh, ay babujee.' I was just about to bite hungrily into a fried sandwich at the Ambala Cantonment bus station canteen when I became aware of this sound behind me, a sort of expiring croak, a supremely successful theatrical sound because when I turned round I saw a starving boy with hands outstretched in supplication, whereas what actually stood there, as I discovered when I had given him a coin, was a nimble, intelligent little boy, who ran around the corner with his money so that he could dispose of it in private. He had a companion operating in the canteen, a little girl dressed in rags and clutching a baby. She would pluck at a man's sleeve while he was eating and it was difficult to ignore her persistent exhortations. A big Sikh dropped a sandwich accidentally and pointed it out to the girl, who snatched it up and scurried away. I followed and saw her give it to a woman sitting by the gate who evidently kept all the takings. When the girl returned she approached me. 'Not me again,' I protested, 'I've just given to that boy.' I still had some difficulty in expressing myself, and this might have made my voice sound harsher than I meant because a man standing nearby, who had successfully ignored the children until now, looked at me stiffly and as he moved away ostentatiously dropped a coin to both the children. No stigma is attached to begging in India because it does not bear the taint of failure or idleness; it is simply a necessary stratagem for remaining on or above the subsistence level.

Behind the bus station Ambala Cantonment stretched out between long broad streets, anathema to the walker, and I had a job to find what I was looking for—St Paul's Cathedral. I had been christened there. I found ruins, a dangerous crumble of masonry and massive beams with just enough form to show that this had been a church of some dignity and size. St Paul's had received a direct hit from a bomb during the 1965 India-Pakistan war, perhaps because of its proximity to troop billets. A tablet in the tower recorded that: 'The flagstaff on the tower of this church was erected AD MCMXX as a mark of thanksgiving to Almighty God for the Victory of the

Allied Arms in the Great War'; and leaning against the chancel wall was a notice painted on a piece of twisted tin nailed to a pole, 'Love is not love which alters when it finds alteration.'

The British association with Ambala Cantonment was military rather than spiritual, however, and the mile on mile of army cantonments still remain as memorial to the British Army tradition. The sentries, the buildings, the hedges, the roads were all smart as if turned out for inspection. When I did find the Deccan Horse Mess, my motor cyclist friend, the lieutenant, greeted me as if he had expected me that very minute, and he had not forgotten the promised bath. Water was heated in a bucket by using an electric element and when the fuse blew, there was the batman to fix everything, to take my clothes round to the regimental dhobi—washerman—and to bring in afternoon tea. Hospitality did not end there. Brushing aside my doubts, my host led me to dinner in the Mess, dressed as I was in the only trousers I possessed, a shirt belonging to my host, and a pair of his sandals, a couple of sizes too big for me. We dined at a large oval table with a silver candelabra standing at the centre and chandeliers hanging from above, off plate bearing the Regimental crest.

The Mess silver was displayed in the Ladies' Room. Round the walls in silver frames were photographs of former British officers, and in glass cases lying on the highly-polished sideboards were medals which they had presented to the Regiment. Other Regimental treasures included signed photographs of King George V, Queen Mary, and Edward, Prince of Wales, and a Mess Book dating from the beginning of the century in which one officer had made the terse suggestion: 'Sack the Cook'.

My host took me some way along the Grand Trunk Road next morning on his motor-cycle, and my departure, though I sat on the pillion with my rucksack on my back, had something of glory in it, because sentries along our route through the cantonments all stiffened to attention and saluted as we sped by. I was left on the road out of sight of Ambala, and once again I had the Grand Trunk Road before me and a clear blue sky above. Few people were on the road. Forestry workers were busy felling thorny acacias marked with the Forestry Department's white cross, and replacing them with rows of eucalyptus saplings. The forestry people were obviously very enthusiastic in this region because a number of large signs had been erected bearing such messages as, 'It is better to have trees than gold in the bank'. Little traffic passed and in half-an-hour all I saw were four bullock-carts and a cyclist with a crate of hens on his carrier.

This was Hariana, a region that had once been part of the Punjab, but was established as a separate state in 1966. As the Sikhs are the major group in India's Punjab, so the Jats, who like the Sikhs are yeoman farmers and much in demand as soldiers, predominate in Hariana.

The major crops in Hariana, as in the Punjab, are wheat, sugar cane and mustard, and though the land in Hariana is reckoned to be somewhat poorer than that in the Punjab, the Jat farmers, like their counterparts in the Punjab, are a relatively wealthy community.

Only a trickle of water was flowing in the beds of the rivers crossed by the Grand Trunk Road between Ambala and the road junction for Kurukshetra at Pipli, but it was sufficient for women who were washing clothes, and for men who in one river bed were washing carrots by churning them with their feet in sloping troughs near the river. Little in the appearance of the countryside I was passing through could have changed in the past century, and old men still alive must remember the days when most of the traffic along the Grand Trunk Road was foot traffic, when, as in *Kim,* travellers would stop for the night at camping places—'paraos'—along the way, finding there everything necessary for the night; a small police station, sellers of fuel and simple food, space to spread a blanket, a small shrine at which to worship and, most important, water from a well. Many of these old sites can still be seen on the stretch of road between Ambala and Delhi. It was somewhere along this stretch of the Grand Trunk Road that Kim and the lama slept on the night before Kim saw the Mavericks pitching camp, found his Red Bull on a green field and came into the care of Mr Bennett and Father Victor.

Lorries were unknown in those days, however, and lorries have their uses. Sikhs dominate the trucking industry across Northern India, and most trucks therefore have an effigy of Guru Nanak painted over the cab, as well as various lucky symbols on the doors, but on the whole these trucks are not nearly so gay as the Pathan trucks of the Western Punjab. I would not have been able to squeeze into a Pathan truck's heavily padded and decorated cab as I now entered the cab of a truck that stopped without my signalling, to sit with my rucksack on my lap beside a policeman, two boys, the driver and his mate. They took me within easy walking distance of Kurukshetra.

Kurukshetra—Kuru's field—is one of the most famous places in Hindu lore, the great field on which the epic battle described in the Mahabharata was fought between the Kauravas (the sons of Kuru) and the Pandavas (the sons of Pandu). Whether a battle of anything like the proportions described was fought, or whether the story was purely of symbolic significance, does not appear to concern the pilgrims who come to Kurukshetra. The Mahabharata, like the Ramayana, is one of the great books of their religion and the story of the battle, which was fought over eighteen days until the Kauravas were finally routed, is a stirring one.

It was on the battlefield of Kurukshetra, before the battle actually started, that Lord Krishna gave a great sermon, which is preserved in the Bhagavad Gita, itself part of the Mahabharata, but often published as a separate book.

The extent of the field, it is generally believed, was about 160 miles in circumference, and on this field, before the battle, tens of thousands of tents were raised for the warriors of each army. Warriors had come from all over the earth, bringing with them elephants and horses, so that when the armies had assembled the rest of the earth appeared to be emptied of men and martial beasts. The opposing warriors shouted with joy when they sighted each other, beating drums and blowing conches. Thunder claps added to the tumult and the earth shook. Then the battle began, with the fighting sometimes continuing far into the night, causing such rivers of blood that the whole field was soaked with it and stained forever. And indeed the soil in this area, as any villager will point out, is of a brownish red colour.

The village of Kurukshetra is only one of many towns and villages on the plain of Kurukshetra today, but it has a special significance because of the peculiar sanctity of the Sanyahet tank, an artificial pool some 1200 yards long. This is considered a holy place for bathing at normal times but especially so during a solar eclipse. Hindus believe that during solar eclipses the Sanyahet is visited by all other tanks in India and by the country's rivers, so that if one happens to bathe in the Sanyahet at the moment of the eclipse one gains the merit of bathing in all the waters of India. As a consequence, Kurukshetra regularly receives some 500,000 pilgrims at each solar eclipse.

Places that are accustomed to visitations by crowds of this size are unlikely to become excited at the arrival of a single stranger, and when I asked about accommodation the rather apathetic citizens of the village seemed indifferent whether I stayed for the night or not; they could, after all, attract enormous crowds without any effort on their part, so there was no need whatever for any form of public relations. They all seemed to be recuperating from the last batch of pilgrims and even the vultures weighing down the branches of the trees seemed to be brooding without much interest in life. The only animation on that still afternoon was shown by three children carrying metal trays, who were following a small herd of buffaloes and hurriedly scraping their deposits off the road. To my surprise I found a room for the night, and a very good one too, in the rest-house of the Kurukshetra Hindu University, a modern villa in a pretty garden quite close to the great tank.

Fewer holy men than I had expected were to be found in the area, but a number of priests, their faces and upper bodies covered with bizarre ochreous markings were living in the crumbling temples that fringed the Sanyahet tank. The sun was nearly setting as I stood beside the water and as the sky coloured, so the pool was burnished and seemed to cover all the surrounding land. As intended by the builders of the tank, the water was conducive to reflection and I was absorbed in thoughts that I would not have been able to analyse when I was startled by a harsh voice asking where I was going. It was a beggar and he and I seemed to be the only creatures by the shining water. I was his boy, he said, his brother, and had I a rupee for him as he had not eaten since breakfast.

Thanesar, one mile away from the sacred tank has a long history, but as a lecturer in Indian History at Kurukshetra University put it to me: 'Well actually, you see, it is very old, but it is not interesting.' Apparently the town had never recovered after being sacked by Mahmud of Ghazni in 1014. A shopkeeper in Thanesar bazaar admitted that there was little to see, but claimed that an underground passage runs from under the mid-sixteenth-century tomb of Shaikh Chilli Jalal in the local fort all the way to Delhi, a hundred miles away. 'You can see the signs pointing to the passage,' he said, 'but it has been closed now.'

He had lived in Thanesar all his life and seemed to believe the legend, and others I asked did not deride the claim. Thanesar has been a battleground for much of its history, lying as it does in the line of advancing armies from the north-west, between the Jumna in the east and the desert in the west, but the remains of the old

Muslim Fort still look as though they can withstand modern artillery, and one can almost believe that the men who built such stout cliff-like walls, could also have built a hundred-mile-long tunnel, had they wished.

An American Peace Corps volunteer working in Kurukshetra was potentially a useful source of local information but it happened that he had attended a wedding feast the previous day, had eaten too many jilaybees and was now lying on his porch miserably repentant. Leaving, I tried to take a short-cut through his garden, split the seat of my only pair of trousers when climbing through a barbed wire fence and spent the next hour with a needle and thread.

Back on the Grand Trunk Road I met a half-wit disguised as a sergeant of police, wearing a heavy khaki overcoat in the afternoon heat. He crossed the road and approached me as I photographed a trio of buffalo herdsmen, and demanded to see my passport. 'It is my duty. India has many enemies. It is my duty.'

Soon afterwards I made a much pleasanter acquaintance, a hale old man with a grey, walrus moustache and a face glowing with goodwill and curiosity, who strode down a dusty lane to the Grand Trunk Road with a stout staff in his hand and a blanket over his shoulders, on his way to take a turn as watch at the family tube-well. He walked as though the world belonged to him, a man who expected respect, but the proud set of his shoulders was tempered by the kindly old eyes. I had taken off my rucksack to ease my shoulders for a while and he stopped for a chat, telling me about the battle of the Mahabharata between the Kauravas and Pandavas as though it had occurred in living memory instead of being part of Hindu lore, an event of about 1500 BC. He pointed out the battle-field with strong brown fingers—so many 'kos' in this direction, and so many 'kos' in that. (The 'kos' as a measurement of distance varies in different parts of India, but in this region it was about a mile and a half). As I listened to him I wondered whether the Christian faith would be stronger in Europe now if the deeds of Christ and his Disciples were written in the countryside of Western Europe instead of in distant Israel and Jordan. When the old man set off across the fields I caught a bus for Karnal, about fifteen miles on, one of the most prosperous cities of Hariana State.

While I had been repairing my trousers in Kurukshetra, the queasy American had brightened enough to tell me about another Peace Corps volunteer, who worked near Karnal in a village called

Kunjpura. 'A very interesting old walled village. Just call there and he will be very glad to put you up and show you around.' I am always wary of hospitality offered vicariously, but nevertheless I decided to visit Kunjpura; I could always return to Karnal later in the evening. Bus services were infrequent, so tongas still plied on the seven-mile route, the charge being a regular sum per head on a shared basis. I shared with nine others plus a large sack of fodder, and sat with my feet dangling over a wheel, while the driver straddled one of the shafts, upwind of me unfortunately. The journey took fifty minutes, and when we arrived the crumbling minarets of Kunjpura town were being coloured by the setting sun.

Until Partition, Kunjpura, a very pretty, traditional little Muslim town surrounded by a wall, was the capital of a small independent Muslim State ruled by a Nawab. It had a fort, attractive mosques with ethereal minarets and fine houses with private wells and mosques; but now Kunjpura is collapsing, the fort is in ruins, the mosques are cow byres and private homes, and there are broad gaps in the walls. The sunset, however, was kind to the town, touched the remaining minarets with pink and gold and imparted a mellow softness to the ruins.

The inhabitants of Kunjpura were very hospitable. The American Peace Corps worker was away for a few days, so the townsfolk decided I was to be their guest. The owner of a teastall that had no better premises than steps by the edge of a street would accept no payment for the tea I drank and a sweetseller's son who happened to be sitting there invited me to stay at his house for the night.

His home was built round a cobbled yard within a high surrounding wall, and because his father specialized in crystallized vegetables the stairways to the upper floors of the house were lined with pumpkins. I shared a room with the sweetseller's son and only learned next morning that his father had slept in his shop in the bazaar: whether this was, as he said, because there had been a number of burglaries in the bazaar lately and he wished to be on guard, or whether, as I suspected, it was so that I could have a bed for the night, I could not discover, but both father and son were proudly hospitable. When I came to the bazaar in the morning the sweetseller was already busy though it was only 7.30 am and a number of customers were crouched round the warm clay oven cradling brass cups of steaming tea. His shop, like the others in the row, had mud walls and was roofed with a thatch of branches and dried mud. It seemed a smoky little shop but had three rooms stretching into the darkness beyond, each illuminated only by the light entering through a hole in the roof.

The morning sun was shining on the rooftops but not yet into the narrow streets, and the scene was not as pleasing as it had been the previous evening, because it was now clear that the ruins were the result of recent neglect and not age. The great door of the fort, with its cruel elephant spikes designed to prevent the use of an elephant as a battering ram, hung incongruously from a small section of sound wall, while round a corner ten yards of once-stout walls were now rubble and used by unfastidious villagers as a public lavatory.

Only seven passengers shared the tonga on which I returned to Karnal. The driver was genial with his passengers but appeared to hate his horse. He was of the rough school, like the Kasur tonga-wallahs, and flicked the horse with the regularity of one keeping time to martial music. 'Gharam hoye, Oh Gharam: Tch, tch, tch.' Flick flick . . .

The French botanist Victor Jacquemont, who travelled in India between 1828 and 1831, said of the interior of Karnal that it was: '. . . an infamous sink, a heap of every sort of uncleanliness. Among heaps of dung, brick-rubbish and concourse of beasts are winding paths scarcely passable for horses, and having here and there a few miserable huts. I have seen nothing so bad in India; and it is fair to mention that amongst the natives its filth is proverbial.'

On entering old Karnal, that part of the city within the old walls, I found myself in what appeared to be a maze, surrounded by half a dozen children who vied with each other in giving wrong directions. Surprisingly, the main street in this old quarter is broad and straight, and walking along it one can see at once who acquires wealth in Karnal; every second modern building along this way bears the brass plate of an advocate (barrister) and the intervening buildings house banks, each guarded by an unlikely-looking guard who might well be an illustration of a pre-war Balkans bandit, with an ancient shotgun and heavily-loaded bandolier. Just off this main road the lanes wind without benefit of town planning. A beggar advanced slowly down a cobbled way, bellowing as he came, a terrifying figure combining in his appearance poverty, degradation and a menacing suggestion of great strength. He moved like a baby that has not learned to crawl properly, on his rump, bearing a baby on one arm, a child on his lap, and a bag for alms in his other hand.

His eyes stared straight ahead and were apparently sightless, the long wild hair about them streaked with sweat and dust. I wondered that the child on his lap, whose feet dragged in the dust, did not leap up and run away in terror; my own instinct was certainly to move towards a less congested way. Women shopping in his line of advance scrabbled in their purses and turned away with tight lips to let the ghastly figure pass. Another beggar, in orange robes, walked through the bazaar at the end of his day, a python curled about his shoulders. Then came the strangest figure of all, a man in a loose green turban and a long, faded red shirt over baggy pants, carrying a large rattle and a megaphone and wearing bells about his ankles which jangled at each stride. He was a rat poisoner and I felt I was back in the Middle Ages.

In the new town, employees of a local bus company were holding a strike meeting in support of their demand for a rise in pay equal to that recently received by Punjab employees of the company. They had punctured the tyres of one of their buses, which now lay with a very dejected appearance at the edge of the bus station square, and a couple of their members were on hunger strike. When I arrived the two on hunger strike were being led away by police and the strikers were being exhorted with a great deal of shouting to maintain their stand. Where few read newspapers or hear news on the radio and where television is non-existent, then those who wish their cause to be widely known must shout. I asked one of the strike officials, a mild-looking Sikh, whether the strike would not hurt the strikers more than it hurt the bus owners and at this his mild eyes hardened. 'We are in the habit of keeping some money aside', he said sharply, 'unlike in the West where people spend their money when they get it.'

A huge banyan tree, a natural arch, spanned the road by the southern end of the old town wall, and passing under this I was in the country again, seventy-five miles north of Delhi, on the direct alignment of Sher Shah Suri's road. Panipat was twenty miles south and I thought I would walk there by evening, but I had not gone half-a-dozen miles before a plump jovial Sikh on a motor-cycle stopped and offered me a lift. I should have walked, for as I straddled the pillion my trousers split again, more extensively if possible than they had done at Kurukshetra, and when we came into Panipat and I dismounted, I could not walk with my usual stride but had rather to move forward with a sort of shuffling motion that must have appeared ludicrous.

A cluster of tea houses and restaurants supported each other alongside the Grand Trunk Road at Panipat and while I sat in one of the teashops I witnessed a scene that might have been the opening of a Communist propaganda drama. A party arrived by car: a tall, fat, forceful man of about fifty, a beautiful young woman with a man who might have been her new husband, and a self-assured, well-fed boy, who all sat at a table set upon a low platform in the open, the focal point of the grimy bazaar. They wore expensive clothes, looked as if they customarily ate well and gave the impression of being wealthy. An old woman carrying a beggar's tin now came shuffling along in front of the stalls, working her toothless gums. On her head she bore a little gunny sack, and when she was near the dining party she stopped, lifted down the sack and rummaged in it with old fumbling fingers, while a ragged boy with a squint who was hanging on to her dirty cotton sari peered up at her. Meanwhile the party of rich diners was enjoying dinner—the older man, especially, was eating with relish, showing his tonsils with every bite, and the old woman, apparently finding nothing in her sack, looked hesitantly up at him and feebly raised her tin. The man went rigid, stopped munching in mid-bite and stared at her, an expression almost of horror on his face. He then barked angrily and gestured her away and she, tying up her gunny sack, shuffled slowly away with the boy following, still holding her sari.

The rent in my trousers made me reluctant to walk far, so I was glad to be told that the best hotel, no, the only hotel in Panipat, was just fifty yards away in this same bazaar row, but I had to walk past it twice before I found it, so humble was the façade. It was built on two floors round a small courtyard, and the design of the rooms was simple but very practical. Brick floors sloped slightly so that water thrown in by the cleaner would drain through a hole in the wall into the street, stout wooden shutters covered the unglazed windows and the furniture was light and almost indestructible.

'You will receive every facility. If you want anything you just stand on the balcony and call Jolly,' said the engaging little Bengali hotel waiter, the first Bengali I had met on the journey.

The old town of Panipat had a peaceful and established air, but its history had been a bloody one, three of the most decisive battles in Indian history having taken place in its vicinity. The first great battle was in 1526, when Babur defeated Ibrahim Lodi, Sultan of Delhi. In 1556 the young Akbar triumphed over Muhammad Shah

Adil, nephew of Sher Shah Suri, thereby establishing the Moghul power. In 1761, in perhaps the most notable battle of all, the combined forces of the great Mahrattas were defeated by the Afghans.

The Patron Saint of Panipat is Boali Kalandar, of whom it is written that he stood in the River Jumna for seven years praying—in those days the Jumna flowed by the town—until the fish had gnawed his legs and he was so stiff that he could hardly move. He then asked the Jumna to move back seven paces and the river, in its haste to obey, moved back seven kos, so that today it flows some twelve miles east of Panipat. He gave the citizens of the town a charm to dispel all the flies from the city, but they grumbled and said that they rather liked flies, so he brought them back a thousandfold. Today, Panipat is noted for its flies, even among Indian cities, but fortunately while I was there it was not the peak fly season.

During my wanderings I came upon a ring of children sitting in a paved lane with their parents ranged behind them, watching a magician, an old man in khaki homespun and a loose turban who carried a little earthenware jar with a short spout in one hand and a stick in the other. He filled the jar with water, then poured out the water through the spout. 'Right?' he asked. 'Right. Now watch this.' He appeared to pass the stick right through the jar so that the ends of the stick were visible at either side. Now he beat a little drum, never stopping his spiel for an instant, while his audience sat enraptured. Water, he said, would now return to the jar, but from where? Should he draw it from the sky? He moved as though drawing water through the air, and a child who had been standing near where he had pointed promptly sat down. The magician beat his drum again, his huge eyes seemed to dilate and the children gasped as slowly he tipped the jar and water streamed out. There was a moment of silence, then the children clapped rapturously and their mothers muttered, 'Yes, it is magic'.

The bustle of the day's business diminished in the late afternoon, the dust slowly settled and the air was sweetened with the scent of incense. Women in ankle-length, many-pleated skirts that swung bewitchingly at each step passed by with water jars on their heads, covering their faces when they saw a stranger. Old men were still working in the open, stringing charpais, their gnarled fingers moving nimbly as they created their patterns with the rough rope. Shopkeepers sat at their door-sills and chatted, happy to point out their wares to me without any notion of selling anything. Though it was a busy town old Panipat had somehow retained the tranquility of a country village.

A Sikh gurdwara across the road from my hotel started broadcasting sacred music at 5 am next morning and at about 6 am I heard the merry tune of *She'll be coming round the mountain* set to Indian words that I did not understand; someone in one of the lower rooms was generously sharing his transistor radio with the other residents of the hotel and I was intrigued to learn later that the lyric was a hit song from an Indian musical.

Sparrows flew in at the door when I opened it to receive my breakfast, and Jolly stopped and chatted till an Army NCO called him from below, addressing him as 'Bengali dada' (Bengali brother). I set off fairly early and was soon in open country. Women with trays on their heads, carrying food to their menfolk, came onto the Grand Trunk Road from the paths that led to villages and some of them walked two miles and more to the cane fields or roadworks where their husbands were working. This was a dry stretch of country and the Persian wheel was in frequent use, powered in some cases by a single camel instead of the more common pair of bullocks, most working in the open instead of in the shade of trees. I began to be uncomfortably hot and was very glad to stop when I came to a wayside teahouse.

I came at length to a small bazaar at the junction of the Grand Trunk Road and the way to a small market town and there, in the shade of neem trees, I found an encampment of Gadolia Lohars, nomadic Rajasthani tinkers who believe that they are descended from Vishwakarma, master craftsman of Hindu Mythology. I had been told that they were to be found roaming all over North India, especially within a radius of a hundred miles of Delhi, doing seasonal work and odd jobs, but this was the first group I had met. They were working inside a circle formed by their beautiful carts—each cart intricately carved with flower patterns—seated around a fire of glowing coals, beating hinges and rough strips of metal into blades and bowls. Both men and women were at the hammers, while one woman worked two leather bags—one held in each hand—joined to a single tube to form a very effective pair of bellows. The men were long-haired, filthy and ragged, but the women wore attractive black dresses embroidered with silver thread and pleated skirts reaching just below their knees. I reached for my camera but the men waved threateningly and adamantly refused to let me take a photograph, though the women smiled boldly, showing fine white teeth.

A little boy brought me my food at a nearby stall, carrying chuppattis in bare hands that a moment before had carried coals for the fire: then he was given food for himself by the proprietor and instead of sitting at one of the tables, he climbed onto the concrete slab above the fuel store in a corner, and squatted there to eat.

I was now about forty miles from Delhi, a formidable distance as it turned out for the asthmatic old bus which brought me before dusk to the bus station near the Kashmiri Gate in the walls of Old Delhi. As the lights in the old Moghul capital were being lit I was ensconced in a room with a balcony in a tiny hotel overlooked by the minarets of the Jama Masjid, a few minutes' walk from the high walls of the Lal Qila, the Red Fort.

10

The sweets in Old Delhi, it is said, are sweeter than those anywhere else in India, and no sweets in Old Delhi are sweeter than those in the shops of Chandni Chowk. There they lie, row on row, succulent piles of colours, made as they were in the days of the Moghuls, pyramids of pure cream and sugar, dripping with juice and stuffed with nuts.

Life could not have been so hard for the Moghuls towards the end if they could order freely from shops like these. But on the whole the last of the Moghuls had a rather lean time.

When Old Delhi, the thirteenth city to rise on Delhi's plain, was built by Emperor Shah Jehan between 1639 and 1648, the Moghul court was one of the wonders of the world and the Red Fort was perhaps the richest palace in the universe, with the Peacock Throne as its star possession. The finest craftsmen in India assembled within the city's red walls. Chandni Chowk running due west from the Red Fort was the main artery of the city, lined with the minor palaces of nobles and generals.

But Moghul power was already waning when Aurangzeb died in 1707 and it was only a matter of time before the riches of Delhi attracted a marauder from beyond the north-west frontier, someone like Timur Lang the Mongol whose troops had sacked Delhi in 1398.

Nadir Shah duly invaded India in 1738 and entered Delhi in 1739. His troops massacred an estimated 100,000 men, women and children, Nadir Shah watching the slaughter from a vantage point in Chandni Chowk. When Shah returned home his booty included the Peacock Throne and the Koh-i-nur diamond.

Less than twenty years later northern India experienced the first raid of Ahmed Shah Abdali, the Afghan, who was to invade India on no less than nine occasions. The most fateful of these nine for Delhi was the fourth, when in 1756/7 Abdali pillaged the city and his booty was humped back to Afghanistan on the backs of 28,000 elephants.

The Mahrattas then despoiled Delhi of what Nadir Shah and

Abdali had left behind, and the Moghul decline lasted until the dynasty ended when the British took over after the Mutiny in 1857.

After the events of the past 200 years a tourist guide should have a plethora of material, but it appears that any tourists who do come to Old Delhi are rushed through the Red Fort, perhaps have a chance to photograph the Jama Masjid, the largest mosque in India, and are then whisked back to their hotels in New Delhi.

Most of the area in the Red Fort that is open to tourists is laid out in lawns and the few remaining Moghul structures are lonely but beautiful museum pieces. The white marble Diwan-i-Khas, the Court of Private Audience, and the neighbouring Pearl Mosque have pure cool lines that are a delight in the summer heat. The famous couplet, 'If there is a paradise on the face of the earth, it is this, it is this, it is this', is inscribed on the wall of the Diwan-i-Khas and this drew sharp comment from Captain W. H. Sleeman when he visited the Red Fort in 1836.

> 'Anything more unlike paradise than this place now is can hardly be conceived,' he wrote. 'Here are crowded together twelve hundred kings and queens [for all the descendants of the Emperors assume the title of Salatin, the plural of Sultan] literally eating each other up . . .
>
> 'Kings and Queens of the house of Timur are to be found lying about in scores, like broods of vermin without food to eat or clothes to cover their nakedness.'

Outside the Red Fort two tourists were listening obediently to a guide who was preparing them for Chandni Chowk. 'This street we will be visiting,' he said, 'is meaning only Moonlight Street and there is a Sikh temple. It is a temple where the ninth Sikh guru was beheaded. The steps are wet and it is very crowded, and I do not think you will be interested in it.'

Undoubtedly these tourists missed the flavour of the noisy and colourful way, where one can spend hours, as I did, exploring the mile-long street and the ramification of alleys—khatras—that run into it.

North of Chandni Chowk is the great red pile of Old Delhi Station, the heart of India's rail system, with lines radiating to all parts of the subcontinent, where there is always a sense of urgency and excitement such as must have prevailed at the great ports of

Europe in the days of sail when an expedition or naval fleet was preparing to leave.

Red-shirted coolies trot along crowded platforms with mountainous loads upon their heads, clearing the way before them with shouts; food vendors push their trolleys between families squatting on the concrete by their baggage, shouting their wares, vying with the coolies for sound supremacy, while Indian passengers rush about looking for friends and lost relatives, also shouting, because no-one could possibly hear if they didn't shout and because it is not in their natures to remain silent.

Most of the long-distance trains leave Old Delhi late in the evening and many passengers waiting for trains curl up in cotton shawls on the platform, apparently asleep in the centre of a noisy babble of agitated passengers seeking friends, and vendors of papers and magazines, foodstuffs, cigarettes and tea, all crying their wares. When a powerful globe of light becomes visible far down the line it is as if an electric current has passed through all those waiting: matrons grasp their children, fathers grip their luggage, coolies hump their loads and everyone, including the apparently mummified figures that have been lying on the platform, rush forward, as with wheels and pistons enveloped in steam the great engine arrives, pulling coach on coach of what must be one of the longest trains in the world.

In front of the station, along the pavement by the street, vendors sell food of the simplest and cheapest kind and their stalls are always well attended by scavengers. One day I saw a man among the scavengers, a tall, thin figure in black underpants and a ragged suit jacket, a shy creature stepping warily and daintily, almost like a gazelle. He sighted a dollop of pulp food on the pavement and leaning over with stiff legs and his rump high, bent his head nearly to the street, and with his fingers flicked the mess into his mouth.

Five minutes later I saw another curious sight when I went to catch a bus. A queue of sorts had formed by a metal railing, but when the bus arrived the queue broke and everyone rushed for the entrance door at the rear. As I strove to overcome a disinclination to shove wilfully like the others I noticed that a man and a girl at either side of the door were making motions of trying to enter, but though they might have boarded did not do so. In the crush I did not get the chance to observe them for long but as I was about to board the bus the girl was still there, her head averted, her sari half covering her face. Instinctively I put my hand to my back pocket and in doing so grasped her hand, which had got there before me. Pressure from behind pushed me in, she wrenched her hand away and when I could glance around again she had gone: fortunately I had had nothing in my back pocket.

To get to New Delhi I hired one of the scooter cabs that ply as busily as flies in Delhi. They are mere boxes built over scooter bodies, with broken springs and meters that rarely work, but they can be hired very conveniently and operate for a moderate charge (though as to this last matter their drivers are very likely to overcharge and it is advisable to check the proper rates before boarding). My driver was skinny and dishevelled, a defeated-looking figure, but I discovered as soon as we were in motion that life still burned feverishly in him. In driving that scooter he unleashed all his frustrations. He was like Mr Toad at the wheel of his car, making game of pedestrians and sending them leaping for the sidewalks, challenging other scooter drivers for passing space and invariably winning the game of nerves. Once he took both hands from the handle-bars to beat his chest while he laughed with crazy joy and sang aloud. I was too fascinated to be afraid, but even so, after we had careered past three stout matrons and just missed two plump bottoms, I was relieved when I alighted, though saddened to think his spirit might now flee him.

New Delhi, the fourteenth of the cities of Delhi, was built by the British to succeed Calcutta as capital of India, and was officially inaugurated in 1930. This is the Delhi of politicians, diplomats, tourists and newspapermen, a spacious city with broad avenues, impressive government buildings and modern hotels, but it lacks the vitality and character of Old Delhi.

New Delhi is a mausoleum at night except in the hotels: Old Delhi by contrast seems reluctant to go to bed. From the balcony of my room at the Hotel Naaz I looked down on a busy way where the lamps of the stalls were lit until nearly midnight and at the Muslim restaurants of the area diners sat and conversed until the early hours. The area, dominated by the 130-foot-high minarets of the Jama Masjid, was a Muslim ward. By day it had a dusty and humble appearance and the little boys playing in the lanes were constantly threatened by the wheels of bullock-carts and tongas. At night, though, the little shops, lit by kerosene lamps and naked electric lights, became romantic caverns, and the men who squatted inanimately in their stalls by day, now surveyed the night with glowing eyes.

11

My status rose considerably after I had made visits to a laundry and a hairdresser in Delhi and when I went to the Interstate bus station to buy a ticket for Aligarh, eighty-three miles away, it was automatically assumed that I would travel first class. I sat between two women, with their three babies, and though I am accustomed to babies—not afraid, that is, that they will disintegrate when I pick them up—I was nervous of these ones because they tended to overlap me and they wore neither pants nor nappies. They proved to be well-trained, however; not one of them urinated in the bus and only one was sick on the floor. The other passengers were quiet and expressionless, very different from the grinning and inquisitive people of the Punjab.

The bus driver was the most animated person aboard, a man with a positive philosophy who never hestitated when he had to make a driving decision. If a tonga ahead was taking up half the road, and a bus was approaching from the opposite direction, but slowing to allow a cyclist to sprint by, our driver would overtake the tonga immediately: his driving technique was that of a man who has placated the gods, and is confident of their support.

The Grand Trunk Road was a much humbler way now than it had been before Delhi, without the side lanes that had characterized it previously, and for long stretches it was even devoid of the shelter of wayside trees. The fields beside the road were much larger now, without the variety of crops that can be seen in the Punjab. This was Uttar Pradesh, the state with the largest population and, after the Punjab, the most prosperous state in India.

Most of the state is in the Upper Ganges Plain and is well irrigated. Wheat and barley and sugar cane are the major crops. It is a state where, as in the Punjab, a very large proportion of the population lives in villages.

Aligarh, the first city of note in Uttar Pradesh that I came to, is divided into two by the railway line to Delhi: on one side is the medieval city of Coil, where the fourteenth-century Moorish traveller

Ibn Battuta had a miraculous escape from bandits, and on the other side are the modern Civil Lines, built in British days. On the one side, narrow cobbled bazaar streets wind to the summit of a hill where the old city was built because mosquitoes plagued the surrounding depressions, and on the other side, straight planned streets are lined with official buildings left by the British and with erstwhile city palaces of the princes of petty principalities in the district, built during the time of the British Raj.

The level-crossing gates across the main road between the old and new towns of Aligarh were kept closed for long periods and consequently there seemed to be a permanent attack on the barriers. Cyclists rushed through the side turnstiles with their cycles lifted above their heads, or pushed their machines under the barrier, where the wire strands had been loosened. A traffic policeman approached the gates while they were closed, and instead of controlling the rush, he charged up with his own cycle and passed beneath the barrier.

The railway station attracted the town's buskers, roadside soothsayers and beggars, and a woman sat completely naked on a rag in the station yard. This woman was about thirty years old, did not seem to be begging and no-one appeared to remark on her presence, though in Europe where people are much more permissive in their attitude to women and dress, she would certainly have been rushed away. Some yards further on was a man sitting by a little wooden cage divided into an upper and a lower portion containing a parrot above and a sparrow below. Two dozen envelopes lay on a sheet before him, containing cards that had various permutations of fortune written on them, and the object of this sideshow was that for a payment of the equivalent of about one old penny one of the birds, preferably the parrot, to which the Hindus attribute soothsaying powers, would descend and pick out the envelope containing the fortune foretold for the customer.

A number of beggars with a very good eye for a pitch were grouped on a narrow pedestrian bridge over the railway lines, many of them showing newly-bandaged limbs, others carrying babies with uncombed hair and enormous eyes. The prince of these beggars was seated with outstretched legs, metal crutches laid either side of him, his body jack-knifed at the waist, so that his bearded face lay nearly flat on the planks; from this position he bellowed pleas and blessings in a terrible voice, which warned people approaching up the far steps that they had better spare their money until they reached him.

It seemed a long way from the traditional society of the streets to the gracious buildings and well-tended lawns and gardens of the Muslim University, famous for its School of Muslim Studies. The other notable buildings in new Aligarh were examples of British Victoriana in the Bombay style, which were surviving remarkably well; they included a handsome clocktower, 'erected in 1893 by voluntary subscriptions collected from the Hindus and Mohammedans of the Aligarh district and named after the late J. H. Harrison, Esq., ICS, at that time collector of the district, in gratitude for many acts of kindness performed by him.'

The Dharma Samaj Graduate College, lying twenty yards on the Coil side of the railways tracks, was listed as a Youth Hostel and there I was allotted the whole bare common room for my quarters for as long as I wished to stay. The students were supposed to be working on post-graduate courses and examinations were imminent, but they made so much noise all evening that I think I could have sat in the corridor practising on bagpipes without disturbing anyone; Indians seem to be impervious to noise and by now it had ceased to trouble me.

That evening after I had followed a wedding procession for an hour, I stretched out on my charpai at the hostel to read, but relays of students approached and catechized me about the standard of living in Britain and not until 10.30 pm was I alone at last in my enormous room. I closed the door and settled down to my book, but after a few minutes someone knocked urgently outside, as if seeking sanctuary from raiders, and several voices cried out roughly for me to open up. 'Oh . . . off', I roared, but opened the door to find the university hostel warden on his rounds with a number of inquisitive students.

I had not asked to be awakened next morning, but at 7 am I was roused by the door being rattled and a hoarse voice demanding to be admitted. It was the chowkidar and I wondered if he had some message from the warden, but he said nothing and I returned to my bed hoping he would go away. He followed me, squatted on my charpai frame and gazed down at me from a distance of about eighteen inches with the expression of a large friendly bird.

'Latreen?' he yelled suddenly.

'Yes, yes, I know where it is,' I assured him.

'Tatti,' he bellowed. I nodded. So that was it. I had not been seen queueing the previous morning at the toilet and the warden had kindly told the chowkidar to ensure that I found it today. The chowkidar had a shawl wrapped about him and sat with the patience of one whose life has included many, many hours of patient squatting. He looked as though he would stay where he was until I did eventually rise and trail to the toilet over by the railway line, but I told him firmly that I wished to sleep, at which he looked disappointed, ruffled his shawl and ambled off. He was a native of Bihar, the first I had met.

Aligarh was the first town in Uttar Pradesh in which I stayed and my chief impression of it was that relations between Muslims and Hindus there were very good, at least when compared with the situation in West and East Punjab and Hariana, where the two communities no longer existed together. When I arrived at the college at Aligarh I had been invited to the house of the Head of the Political Science Department for a cup of tea and he, having enquired about my journey so far, had asked about my early impressions of the town.

'That the local mosques seem to be in good repair and used for worship,' I had replied. 'Nearer the border mosques are used for dwellings and cow-byres.'

'No, no, that is not so,' he exclaimed.

I assured him that I had just come from the north, but he shook his head.

'No, that is not so! You could not have been there.'

He had never travelled far from Aligarh himself, but assumed that I was fabricating a story, which I took as a reflection on his fellows and on the liberal and elastic view that is held of the truth in India. This professor was a charming man, and apparently unaware that he might have been uncivil by implying that I was a liar.

The Grand Trunk Road between Delhi and Kanpur was not shown as a main road on modern maps and this 260 miles of its length seemed to have been forgotten, perhaps because no major town or area was being developed in between. Near Aligarh the road dwindled to a pitted strip of tarmac just wide enough for a single truck to pass along it, with verges of untarred bricks a yard wide and then dust. The land on either side was for some way what the locals termed 'jungle', that is uncultivatable, because salt had risen to the surface. Only a few moribund neem trees stood by the road and they were marked with the government's white cross, which meant that they were doomed to be felled. The absence of trees and the dry land meant that there were no birds. Little traffic passed so this was the quietest stretch of the road I had yet been on: it certainly could not be compared with the lovely land of the Punjab.

The barren patch did not last long, and even on the road through the salty desert I was cheered by the sight of an occasional ekka (a primitive pony-trap), each laden with ten and more passengers, and looking like E. H. Shepard's illustration for the chase of Mr Toad in *The Wind in the Willows*. Several old, disused wells by the wayside now served no purpose and as their surrounding walls were almost flush with the road they must have been a constant hazard at night. Sometimes I would find such a well with no parapet at all lying right in the middle of a path beside a field; it would have been folly to wander out at night without a light. Reports like the following are not rare in the Indian press:

> 'The bodies of a woman and her two sons were found in a well at Puprawat village, four miles from Najafgarh, today.
>
> 'Shakuntla, 30, had gone to a field with her two sons, aged three and five years, for harvesting yesterday. The younger boy fell into a well which had no parapet. The elder boy tried to save his brother but slipped into the well. The mother jumped in to save the boys but lost her life, villagers said.
>
> 'Police had been asked to hold an inquest.'

I now wore a white cotton cap and had the long peak pulled well forward to keep the sun out of my eyes, but even so I was troubled by the glare of light reflected off the road. I would have welcomed a ride in a bullock-cart, but all the carts were going the opposite way, towards Aligarh. For an hour I saw nobody, but a small building, which had once served as a police post and shop, and a nearby well and a shrine were reminders of the days when the Grand Trunk Road had carried considerable foot traffic. Then I heard a minatory 'Hey!' but there was nothing in sight except fields of wheat. 'Hey!', it sounded again. It was a farmer, stalking about amongst the long wheat, frightening away birds as he examined his crop. A short way further on a woman stood in a wheatfield swinging a rope to which a rock had been tied, and she too shouted periodically. Neighbouring farmers had opted for scarecrows, small wooden structures, evidently made without the enthusiasm that goes into making some of the horrifying images commonly found in Indian towns at festival times.

In the Punjab a traveller along the Grand Trunk Road rarely has to go very far before he finds a tea-stall or small restaurant; it is not necessary there to carry food and drink with one, but in this part of Uttar Pradesh the few villages that lay near the Grand Trunk Road rarely had even a tea-vendor. I was hungry and thirsty and, hearing from people going in the opposite direction with bundles on their heads and under their arms that a big weekly market was being held at Nanaupull, a short way further on, I pressed forward eagerly, but on reaching the market I could obtain nothing more than a cup of tea unless I fancied a lunch of dried chillies. The majority of people brought their food with them or stoked up like camels before starting out for the day.

An ekka driver with nine passengers on his vehicle had no hesitation about accepting me as the tenth, and tied my rucksack on at the back; and so I came the two miles into the village of Akrabad, beside the Grand Trunk Road, just thirteen miles from Aligarh.

It was quite a large village, with a wide main street, a stall where I could get a hot meal, and a sweetseller's shop. I was very hungry and, sitting at a flimsy table on a wooden platform behind the broad clay oven, I attacked a meal of chuppattis and curried vegetables while the proprietor squatted gravely by the oven, conversing in a low voice with other customers, but ever attentive to my needs: the poorest man is a king at a roadside 'dhabbar' in India.

After the meal I decided to catch the bus to Etah, the next large town, because by mid-afternoon I always began to be anxious about a bed for the night. I was assured that the bus would arrive at any minute but the minutes multiplied and it became obvious that local bus services were very infrequent. It would soon be the hour when men are prone to fancies engendered by the closeness of the night and will regard a stranger with hostility, but in Akrabad I was accepted. Janki Prasad, the bazaar sweetseller, invited me over to his stall for a cup of tea and within a minute had offered me a bed in his home for the night. As soon as I was his guest all his friends offered their help too: the young postman showed me around the two neighbouring villages before nightfall; two Jat farmers insisted that I stay with them next time I passed this way; the seller of fried grains and pulses, whose wares were easily held by a wicker basket and whose shop was the open dusty way beside the street in front of the sweet-stall, pressed me to eat a mound of gram carefully spiced and served upon three banyan leaves fastened together to form a plate.

In a side-street opposite Janki Prasad's stall was a bangle factory—one of four in the village—lit only by the light from the low, flat, octagonal furnace. Each man working there sat on the floor by a tiny door in the furnace wall and made bangles by heating the special clay and spinning it deftly round on a conical rod. All the workers were Muslims, some old grey-bearded men peering through steel-rimmed spectacles, others boys of little more than fourteen years. They earned three rupees a day and worked from 8 am till 11 pm. They had two days in the week free, not by choice, but because they were having difficulty in obtaining raw materials. Most of the bangles they made were sent to Aligarh, others were sold in markets like that I had seen at Nanaupull. A substantial number of bangles sent away must have been wasted through breakage, because they were packed in gunny sacks without any padding at the sides. The retailer of bangles for the village was a short-sighted old Muslim with a goatee beard, whose stall also stocked peanuts and gram. He was no salesman and watched neither his wares nor passers-by, so he was no match for the crows that perched nearby and filched nuts from his pile. His daughter came out to grind gram in a large stone bowl and chided him for not using his stick when dogs nosed near his baskets and the birds stole. He blinked into alertness, but only for a few moments before returning to the book he had been reading through dirty-lensed glasses. His daughter was beautiful, a sight to turn anyone from the Grand Trunk Road, but she soon disappeared into the house and did not emerge again.

Janki Prasad worked for just as long each day as the bangle-makers, starting at 7 am and finishing at 10 pm without a break between and never a day off, according to himself, in the whole year. All day he squatted by his clay oven, making tea and chatting, and in the evenings he made the sweets for the morrow by the light of a naked bulb. Akrabad had been electrified five years earlier, but only a few shops and fewer houses had electricity, and he was one of the fortunate few. Neither of the neighbouring villages had electricity or running water. When he finished work at last and we stepped off the main street, the way was in pitch darkness. No moon shone overhead, but the stars were more brilliant than they ever are above the cities in Europe.

It was nearly eleven when we came at last to his mud-walled house, which was lit by a single kerosene lantern. Bedding had been laid out on two charpais in a little outhouse across a small courtyard from the main residence and here his wife brought me food. They wanted to converse with me but I fell asleep the moment my head touched the pillow and slept soundly through the night.

I started out next morning with one eye partially closed as the result of mosquito bites. A haze shrunk the horizon and so magnified a temple standing half-a-mile away over the fields that I set off in some excitement through the wheatfields to investigate it, only to find that though it was a large temple for so isolated a spot, it was not nearly as large as it had appeared from the road.

An open-billed stork which seemed to be regarding its reflection in the water of a nearby pond let me approach to within twenty yards before it took off. Soon afterwards I saw three sarus cranes, the largest birds of India, each nearly five feet high and an alarming sight when magnified by the mist. These birds enjoy popular protection in India because they are reputed to mate only once and to remain faithful to their partners throughout their lives.

When Joseph was assisting the Pharoah in Egypt, he must have seen grain carts that differed little from the contraptions which strained towards me after I had returned to the road. They were wooden grain carts, each pulled by a camel, their front wheels half the diameter of the rear wheels, their shafts rising at an angle of 45°, their high walls covered with jute sacking. The only thing Joseph might have found strange about the scene was my camera and perhaps the aggressive tone with which the carters, who had obviously been photographed before, demanded baksheesh.

No-one I talked to about Etah, headquarters of the district next to Aligarh, had any doubt about the town—it had nothing to recommend it. Even the locals confirmed this. I was intrigued when I arrived there by bus to find that many of the men in the bus station carried rifles or steel-tipped quarter-staffs. One man said that men of remote villages usually carried sticks because of the menace of wolves; another said that this district was troubled by dacoits (highway robbers). I had heard in the Punjab that dacoits operated in Uttar Pradesh almost with impunity, because the leaders—so it had been boasted to me—were Punjabis, forced from their own state but very capable of eluding the Uttar Pradesh police. I had been assured, when I had visions of being stripped and robbed and left by the wayside like a latter-day Joseph Andrews, that dacoits would not attack a single traveller: they worked for much bigger stakes, did not hesitate to murder and derived considerable income from protection money levied from the villages.

The Etah dak bungalow stood alongside the Grand Trunk Road. It did not look comfortable from the outside, but I was given a large room for my own use and had my own back-yard with a pump and a banyan tree. The only place of interest in Etah was the local produce market and here I saw a good illustration of the fact that one does not need a shop-stall or many wares to set up business in India. A boy of about twelve went from stall to stall at the centre of the market collecting rotten fruit, furry green oranges, unsightly apples, black and squelchy bananas, till his wicker basket was full. He then staggered over to a space between two bicycle wheels against an open drain, crouched in the dust, deftly rearranged the rotten fruit so that all the colour which yet remained was turned to the front of the basket, and cheerfully started shouting his wares. Soon, incredibly, he had a prospective customer who squatted in the dust beside him, bargaining.

Bewar, the next town, was forty-six miles away along the Grand Trunk Road. The bus I travelled on next day was the ideal vehicle for touring, because it shook one into attention at every few yards, unlike the deep-sprung modern touring coaches in which passengers are divorced from the countryside they pass through. My companions were a father and son returning to their village after a short visit to an aunt at Etah. The little boy had kajal—lamp black—round his eyes, and wore a green jacket with a bright blue button, a dirty shirt which was in holes, baggy shorts made of pyjama material reaching well below his knees and plimsolls without laces, spotted with different colours. Father was a shabbily-dressed but proud-looking man with a curling moustache, and he carried a transistor radio, the symbol of prosperity and progress in India. The boy looked alternately from his father's face to the radio, a smile of adoring wonder on his face.

After a bus ride I was usually delighted to stretch my legs and at such times would have been delighted to find a companion who walked at my pace. At Bewar I dined, walked quickly through the main bazaar, then set off on foot for Nabiganj, seven miles away, in company with a shopkeeper from that township, a young man of about twenty who had decided to join me and who proved an irritating companion. He decided to educate me. 'That is a bullock-cart,' he would say and, 'he is a shopkeeper'. I told him that I had travelled on this road from Peshawar but this had no effect. He called out to acquaintances waiting for the next bus on the outskirts of Bewar that here was a traveller who spoke very indifferent Hindustani and his acquaintances tagged on to enjoy the show. I soon found I was leading a company of eight pedestrians and three cyclists. Each time that I asked a question they would confer together and agree that I did speak very poor Hindustani, and I could never get a satisfactory answer. People we met en route were as profitless. We stopped at a school after a few miles at the request of the teacher, who ran out into the road to stop us. Solemn-eyed children gathered around me without a smile between them; smiles had been at a premium during the last two days. I tried to describe the mechanism of the camera, so that I could gain the children's interest and photograph them.

'Yes, yes, I know that very well,' exclaimed the teacher impatiently. I told him that I was trying to explain to the children, not to him.

'They do not understand your language,' he said stolidly. I began to doubt whether I had ever managed to communicate with anyone in India.

The Grand Trunk Road here was only nine feet broad and very cracked. Traffic held to the centre of the way to avoid the deep dust on either side and when vehicles passed they raised a cloud of dust that hung in the air for over a minute. A marriage party travelling to Bewar in a string of bullock-carts came slowly down the middle of the road, each cart covered with a canopy, the bullocks and carts decorated with strips of coloured cloth. The passengers were all dressed in their best clothes. A bus now approached from the opposite direction, going at full speed, and there was no question of the mechanized giving way to the animal-drawn as the bus held its course; the string of carts pulled over into the dust. No truck would have made way for the bus, and the driver was making the most of a moment of triumph. Soon after this an ekka approached us at a sprightly pace carrying a corpse which was wrapped in a white cotton sheet and bound to the platform, probably on its way to the Ganges.

The people of Nabiganj no sooner saw their colleagues—those who had accompanied me from Bewar—talking to a stranger than they pressed forward curiously and within a couple of minutes of my arrival I was the centre of a crowd of over a hundred people. I was glad of the diversion offered by an elephant that swung down the Grand Trunk Road towards us, its brow painted with chalk, its mahout a thin, hungry-faced man, with eyes like a bush baby's. Where was the elephant going? No-one seemed to know, and I could not understand the mahout's language, but it appeared that the elephant belonged to a rich farmer of this vicinity who kept it for prestige, hiring it out sometimes for wedding processions. Occasionally the mahout made a few annas by giving rides to children in the villages and he needed no persuasion to stop his charge when he saw me. Bringing the elephant to its knees, he dismounted and held out its tail as a step so that I could mount. We promenaded up and down the road for about five minutes, watched by the crowd. When I asked if I might dismount the mahout shrewdly returned that I should pay him first; with my head high up on a level with the branches of the roadside trees I would have been in no position to deny him, even had I wanted to do so.

It had been pleasant to sit aloft for a few minutes above the heads of the people of Nabiganj. When I dismounted I was surrounded again and soon became restive at the close attention of the crowd. I wanted to leave by bus and went to the bus ticket clerk who was sitting by the entrance of a shop to ask about bus schedules, only to be pushed away by the furious shopkeeper who evidently feared that the crowd following me would damage his goods. Someone assured me that the bus would arrive within the hour, but I clambered onto the few square inches of space left on the first ekka going out on the Grand Trunk Road in the direction of Kanpur.

The ekka was bound for Chhibramau, seven miles away, and the sun was sinking when we reached there two hours later, after two altercations between the ekka driver and dismounting passengers. Altercations in these parts followed a ritual: disputants shouted at one another, neither making any effort to see the other's point of view, both working themselves rapidly into a rage so that their eyes protruded and neck muscles bulged. Any foreigner witnessing such a scene for the first time would suppose that homicide was imminent, but both parties continued like this only when they were certain that they would be restrained by their companions, or by bystanders.

When arms were raised, then the disputants were held back and they would immediately struggle to break loose, without, however, exerting quite enough force to free themselves or to give their companions, who themselves argued vehemently, cause for much exertion. Finally both parties would separate and discuss the dispute volubly for hours. The disputes between the ekka-wallah and his passengers were relatively brief, but even so by the time we reached Chhibramau in the dusk I felt that I was adrift and not quite in control. I had already come too far for one day but locals said there was no hotel or inn in this town, nor dak bungalow. I was lucky to catch the last bus for Kanauj, a town with a proud history, but one that had suffered the price of medieval glory by frequent sackings.

It was a cheerless ride in the dark and the passengers eyed me askance. 'Who is this traveller who travels alone at night?' I heard one say.

'Who knows where these people go and when they travel?' replied another. We arrived in darkness at Serai Mirah, a bazaar on the Grand Trunk Road two miles from Kanauj.

The locals were unhelpful. Hotel? Dak bungalow? Not in these parts. What did a fellow who was carrying his own luggage want with a hotel anyway? Fortunately the North Eastern Railway has a station at Serai Mirah and I settled down for the night in the 'Upper Classes' restroom' on a long chair with a hardboard base and armrests five feet long. Mice ran about boldly and kept mounting my pack and the third class passengers peered in at the door, but after midnight mice and men settled and I slept. In the morning I could see that Serai Mirah was a chastened-looking row of impermanent stalls, not a place where one could expect many smiles even by daylight.

The Grand Trunk Road was now only seven miles from the Ganges and at places on the way to Kanpur would approach to within two miles of it. The river dominated the region, geographically and emotionally; even I was constantly aware of it though I had not yet seen it. It seemed to draw men's thoughts as powerfully as if it were the sea, this river of sacred water; to the people it was the beginning, the blessing, the water in which one communed with one's gods and which one joined at death. Bottles of holy Ganges water were no rarity now and wherever I stopped I found someone who was about to go to the river or had just returned from it.

After a walk of about four miles I came to a tea-stall where the vendor was just fanning his fire to start work for the day and he said he could provide breakfast. He had a good site for his business, at a junction of the Grand Trunk Road and a side road leading to the Ganges. I felt that one could do worse than sit in the shade of his shop, serving a few customers, gossiping and watching passers-by. A few men wandered up and eyed me critically. 'The Americans are bigger,' one of them observed at last. The others nodded, Yes, the Americans were rather stronger. The teashop man worked slowly on my breakfast, frying the eggs in his own way, beating them in fat and serving them like a fragmented omelette. The charge staggered me, for the eggs alone cost one rupee each.

By 10 am it was hotter than it had been in the Punjab at noon just two weeks earlier, and when I had walked a few more miles I succumbed to the exhortations of an ekka driver and topped up the load of his vehicle. The condition of the road was now poorer than ever, and a number of trucks stood by the wayside, either with a wheel removed or with a punctured tyre.

Riding on an ekka was very restful and satisfying, even though I usually had to sit either with a leg stuck out stiffly so that it did not touch the wheel, or with my knees under my chin; I could sit undisturbed, musing, excited by the sway of the cart and the insecurity of my posture, yet lulled by the clopping of the horse's hooves on the tarmac. The ekka's destination was Araul Makanpur, just forty miles from Kanpur. The people in this region were smaller than those in the north-west, less communicative, less martial, showing less awareness of the West and its culture. Araul Makanpur was a small village where the sweetseller sold very poor quality 'burfees' that were excessively heavy and seemed to consist of unmelted sugar.

A barber sat on the bricked edge of the road and he and his customers were covered with the dust raised by passing lorries. Flies were spread thickly on the sweet-stalls and birds were active in the trees above, spattering one customer near me and fouling the glass of tea he had just received. A puppy with a prominent ribcage squealed as it was beaten for nosing in a stall and it ran across the road to nose in the dust near me, scuffling amidst peanut shells for any possible morsel of food; but competition was too strong, lean older dogs had already passed that way and little that is edible falls to the ground in India. It crossed the road again and foraged under a couple of fruitsellers' barrows; it avoided the feet of one man who stepped backwards, but could not escape the stick of a passing elder who whacked it indignantly and shooed it across the road, from habit, it seemed, and not malice. The puppy peered at another stall on my side of the road, but was chased away and again it crossed the road. Five minutes later it ran over to my side yet again, squealing and limping, just as a lorry bore down, and somehow, miraculously, the wheels missed it. Within seconds it was questing again, nose down in the thick dust. I lost sight of it then. Another puppy, barely two months old, now appeared opposite me nosing towards a basket by the road, but a stick wielded by a bystander descended on it, and it wriggled away squealing and seemed to be trying to hide itself in the dust. It stopped, squealed in terror a moment later as a hawk swooped low over it, then wriggled along in the dust for a few more yards until it cried out in terror anticipating a blow from the man who now passed it a yard away. Soon afterwards this puppy too disappeared and I did not notice it again. It was no wonder that the adult dogs were lean as greyhounds, with sharp noses and eyes like death, but their skins at least were better than those of most of the pariah dogs that I had seen in Uttar Pradesh, free of the pink spread of mange.

A number of sun-baked earth ramps are a feature of the landscape in this region, and a few miles beyond Araul Makanpur I learned what they signified.

A farmer led two bullocks to the top of a ramp about five feet high and twenty feet long, then smacked the animals to set them running down the slope. The bullocks were harnessed to a large leather bucket by a stout rope that passed over a pulley and down into a well at the head of the ramp. As the animals reached the end of their run in a dip beyond the ramp, so the bucket, filled with water, came to the surface, and a lean old man deftly tipped the water into an irrigation channel. It seemed a very laborious system and one that was wasteful of labour. Evidently the water here lay too far beneath the surface for a Persian wheel to be used and the farmers here were too poor to be able to afford tube wells.

A few high-laden trucks passed on the Grand Trunk Road and sometimes they would slow to permit men waiting by the way to board them. The truck-drivers were running an unofficial bus service, charging two rupees for the ride to Kanpur, the same as the bus fare, but I had been warned that there was no reasonable certainty when the trucks would reach Kanpur, that if the driver wished to stay the night somewhere en route, he would have no compunction about doing so. When a truck stopped and I was offered a free ride to Kanpur, however, I took it and we puttered into the sprawling manufacturing city without incident.

Kanpur has neither history nor beauty to commend it, but succeeds very well without these attributes as a leading manufacturing city with a population noted for their single-minded application to business.

For the British, Kanpur, or Cawnpore as it was more commonly spelled, has a melancholy significance. Today the Sati Chaura Ghat at the Ganges presents a pretty scene as bathers gather there by the temple, but in 1857, during the period of the Mutiny, it was the scene of a massacre. It was here that survivors of the Siege of Kanpur came under an amnesty to board barges that would, so they had been promised, take them to Allahabad. When the Europeans boarded the barges they were fired upon by mutineers who had taken up their vantage points on land two hours previously. Some 125 women and children were taken alive to be kept as hostages, but they were later killed and their bodies thrown down a well. The European contingent at the start of the Siege of Kanpur had numbered 465 men and 280 women and children, but not one survived to welcome Havelock's relieving forces.

I arrived early enough in the second-class waiting room at the station to get a bench to sleep on, and soon the other benches and the floor were occupied by respectable-looking citizens who might or might not have intended to catch a train later that evening or in the morning. I had no difficulty whatever in waking at 5 am and was the first customer at the tea-stall, chatting to the stallholder as he stoked the fires. Early as I was, I was soon joined by a beggar-boy, whose bleary eyes indicated that he was unwillingly afoot, awakened perhaps by a more ambitious and watchful parent or professional guardian. He quickly struck the right professional note: 'Babujee . . . babujee.' I gave him a coin and he turned away, apparently stretching and scratching himself, and when he turned back his hands were empty.

Mist softened the outlines of Kanpur. Half a dozen rickshaw boys were huddled in a circle in the station yard, gambling, their shawls still wrapped about their shoulders for it was a fresh morning. A policeman ambled towards them, an unimpressive, thin-shanked, middle-aged man with a shawl wrapped around his head, and the

12 Dhobis by the Ganges at Benares

13 A worshipper at dawn at Benares

14 Ekka in Benares

rickshaw lads grinned guiltily, humouring him, delighting in the apparent self-abasement which in India is more mischievousness and the acting of a well-understood rôle than servility. The policeman grasped two of the boys and shook them gently, at which one boy, with mock contrition, showed him the few coins that had lain in the kitty: it was an offer, the policeman pocketed the coins and moved away, and those of the corps of rickshaw-wallahs who had witnessed the incident smiled delightedly.

Potential Western beats could learn much about style from the Indian beats who sleep on the broad pavement area near the third class booking hall of Kanpur station. At dawn they were still huddled in their few rags, waiting for the sun to gain strength and heat the pavement so that they could then stretch out for the day. They seemed indifferent to the world and its effort, their bodies unwashed, their hair tangled and long, their clothing minimal: they were the ultimate beats, people who probably had never had the chance to develop a conscious philosophy of negative thought, beats in a land where poverty is the norm and rarely excites any feeling in an observer.

Kanpur and Allahabad districts, with their respective headquarters in cities of the same name, are both prosperous. In between them lies the district of Fatehpur with its headquarters in Fatehpur town, forty-seven miles from Kanpur on the Grand Trunk Road. I arrived there by bus in the afternoon.

It was evident that Kanpur and Allahabad channel off all Fatehpur's wealth, for the town has a very decrepit appearance. Perhaps the general state of collapse dates back to the Mutiny when many buildings in Fatehpur were demolished by rebels.

It was in Fatehpur that R. T. Tucker, the 'Fighting Judge', made his stand during the Mutiny. The British community had taken shelter in the home of the magistrate and deputy collector but Judge Tucker refused to leave his home and would not join the British party when they left the town. He was besieged and was only overcome after a long resistance from the roof of the Courthouse, and then only when the building was set on fire. His bravery that day was equalled by two local Hindus. In a report on the death of the judge the Commissioner of Allahabad wrote: '. . . Mr Tucker, by his earnest and open profession of religion, and by his unbounded pecuniary liberality, had commanded the respect, if not the affection of a large number of the inhabitants of the city, and when the excited mob returned from his slaughter, two Hindus of the town stood out before them and reviled them as the murderers of a just and holy man; it is scarcely necessary to add that they immediately shared his fate.'

Perhaps the most attractive building in Fatehpur is the PWD inspection bungalow and I had this to myself for the night.

Entering Allahabad next day was like coming into a film producer's idea of an Eastern bazaar. Beyond a tall gate in the city wall is the Khuldabad Serai, built by the Emperor Jehangir, and beyond that a bazaar as busy as Old Delhi's Chandni Chowk. Coolies pushed their way through the concourse, their high loads standing like islands above the hundreds of moving heads; blacksmiths in a row of sooty forges wielded their great hammers as if competing for prizes, the urgent metallic beat making the pace for the crowd that pushed in all directions. Above all the clamour rose the shouts of four men who moved forward as a well-drilled team, carrying above their heads a flimsy bamboo stretcher on which lay a long thin bundle wrapped in red cotton stuff—a corpse.

Allahabad's main claim to fame is its proximity to one of the holiest places in the Hindu world, the Sangam, confluence of the Ganges and the Jumna.

Early each year the Magh mela, a month-long religious fair, is held on the sands near the Sangam, and every twelfth year the Kumbh mela, held by rotation every three years at four holy Hindu cities, is celebrated here. Crowds gather for both festivals but especially for the latter. A cluster of pilgrims can be found at the Sangam at any time. When I arrived a substantial number of the beggars and boatmen on the sands made a sortie towards me and made the possibility of any sort of spiritual experience very remote.

With Benares only seventy-eight miles away, few travellers would be likely to spend long in Allahabad, and accordingly after only one night in the city I boarded a bus for the holiest of all cities of the Hindus.

At our first halt we were confronted by a Brahmani bull, a great humped beast which looked as heavy and as dangerous as a rhino, and which snorted with anger when the bus did not flee before its belligerent stare. A number of onlookers soon gathered and the bull turned and lowered its horns at them but it did not leave the bus, and after a minute or so of glowering silence it lunged at one of the mudguards and tried to wrench it off with its horns: it was of a breed held sacred by the Hindus and could afford to be arrogant.

'Jao, Maharaj, jao'—'Go away, great King, away', the conductor pleaded from a window, while the now distant crowd watched the confrontation with great respect, no-one expressing any indignation or alarm that such an animal had been permitted to wander about the streets. Our own driver looked apologetic when we moved away as though sorry that the bus had been the cause of the bull bumping its head.

The little houses in the villages we passed had a neat, prosperous appearance, with smooth walls and tiled roofs. Many of the houses were new, and fellow passengers explained that they were made with mud and disintegrated rapidly, so that a man would be lucky if he did not have to rebuild his home at least once a year.

We had left Allahabad soon after mid-day and made good time to Benares, arriving there in mid-afternoon.

12

Hindus believe that Mayya Ganga, Mother Ganges, has the power to wash away their sins. Over the years special facilities have been provided along the Ganges for pilgrims. Ghats—steps leading down to the water—have been built and temples have been endowed.

The most famous sites along the Ganges include Hardwar and Rishikesh near the upper reaches of the river where the water is still relatively pure in the chemical sense, the Sangam where the Jumna joins the Ganges, and Benares. Of these, Benares is the most famous, a city where Hindu rajahs have over the centuries invested heavily in the construction of ghats and temples.

It is obligatory on Hindus to visit Benares at some stage of their lives, and the best assurance a Hindu can have of a life after death is to die in Benares.

As a consequence Benares probably sees more of the drama of Hindu life than any other city. It is always crowded with pilgrims; and has more priests than any other Indian city. Sunrise and sunset are considered the most auspicious times for bathing in the Ganges at Benares, and I arrived at the ghats of the city just as the sun tipped over the rim of the horizon. The period of dusk is short in the tropics and within a few minutes the lamps were being lit along the water's edge, and the river seemed as broad as a sea in the gloom, reflecting at its edge the paraffin lamps along the ghats, the flambeaux of priests performing prayer ceremonies and the little butter lamps that worshippers launched upon the water.

Clusters of men and women stood by the river or splashed in its waters, engrossed in rituals, bathing, chanting, beating gongs and cymbals, waving flaming torches, worshipping in many cases with a lack of inhibition that seemed to border on hysteria. Impressive as this was, I gathered that there would be a bigger and more colourful turn-out of pilgrims in the morning. And so it proved. As first light tipped the edge of the sand dunes across the Ganges, I came with Hans and Dieter, two young German travellers whom I had met the previous evening, to the Dasashwamedh (Ten Horse Sacrifice)

Ghat, which marks the place where the god Brahma is believed by Hindus to have performed a Ten Horse Sacrifice. The Dasashwamedh is the main ghat at Benares, a place of very special sanctity. And it is no wonder that this is so: a Horse Sacrifice involving one horse, if performed by a god, would have been a momentous event, let alone a Ten Horse Sacrifice.

The Horse Sacrifice (one horse) appears to have been a very special rite performed by ancient kings of India for the purpose of extending their dominions, or for ensuring the birth of a son, or to atone for a sin.

Such sacrifices were extremely rare, because only a king who was very sure of his power would perform one, and because more than a year was needed if the proper rituals were to be performed.

The horse to be sacrificed would be a young stallion, and preferably white, the mystical significance of the animal being that its swift power would be transferred to the sacrificer. The horse would be bathed and decorated in an initial consecration ceremony lasting three days and then it would be set loose, to wander at will. It was recommended that at an early stage in these preliminaries a four-eyed dog be clubbed to death: and if such a dog was not available, then one with marks above the eyes would do.

The horse, having been set free, should be allowed to wander for a year, and if the purpose of the horse sacrifice was aggrandizement, the animal would be accompanied by a small army of princes and retainers, for wherever the horse went, that land was claimed for the king who was making the sacrifice. In the event that territory was disputed, a battle would ensue.

If all went well the horse would be brought back at the end of the year and prepared for sacrifice. Several hundred small animals would be killed first, and then a cloth would be put out for the horse, the animal would be quieted in some way and laid out on the cloth, and then killed, possibly by some form of asphyxiation. After a number of rites, one of the king's wives would be required to lie down beside the dead animal and a top cloth would be laid over cadaver and queen.

It appears that the dead horse was believed to have achieved a divine status and according to the Satapatha Brahmana, one of the holy books of the Hindus, the sacrificer would proclaim, 'In heaven ye envelope yourselves', and the queen, under the cover, would cry something to the effect, 'May the vigorous male, the layer of seed, lay seed,' and go through some reproductive ritual. The ceremonies then concluded with ribald dialogue between the king and the women present at the sacrifice.

Why the god Brahma should have performed a Ten Horse Sacrifice is not clear. One story has it that he had performed a Horse Sacrifice at Prayag (the old name for Allahabad) thereby making the gods, whose home was Benares, jealous. Brahma accordingly performed a Ten Horse Sacrifice at Benares, making it even holier than Prayag.

Another legend has it that Divodas, an early and famous king of Benares, had banished the gods, including the great god Shiva, from the city. After some while, Shiva asked Brahma to bring him news of the city, and so Brahma went to Benares, built a home there, and changed himself into an ancient Brahman. Mindful of the need to enable the gods to return to Benares, Brahma conceived the idea of tricking Divodas into committing a sin—one of omission—which would prove him unworthy to rule the city so that he would have to leave.

Brahma accordingly asked for ingredients for an extremely complex sacrifice, and it seemed unlikely that Divodas would be able to provide what was required. The king, however, produced sufficient not just for one, but for ten sacrifices which Brahma duly performed, including in each instance a horse in the sacrifice. Why he should have done this, and whether the rituals were anything like those for the Horse Sacrifice already described is not clear. The sacrifices ensured the very special sanctity of the place where they were performed and it is not surprising that the Dasashwamedh Ghat should be one of the busiest in Benares.

Soon after the arrival of Hans, Dieter and myself at the ghat in the early morning, the pink rim on the horizon rapidly broadened and suffused the lower sky and within minutes the incandescent stars had lost their glow and the dark pall of the night sky turned perceptibly blue. On the lowest steps along the ghat some worshippers faced the East, holding brass lotas (jars) of water before them, and as the sun rose they poured the water into the river, praying as they did so. Some worshippers set to beating gongs frenziedly, and to blowing horns; some jumped into the river, laving themselves, diving under the water a prescribed number of times; and some even sipped the water. Others sat quietly at the water's edge with their gleaming brass vessels arrayed beside them. Some women plunged into the water with their saris draped coyly about them, others bathed with their breasts bare. All seemed utterly absorbed in their ritual. Unmoved by all the devotion around them, the priests sat watchfully on concrete platforms built against the steps of the ghat, shouting and gesticulating when they saw us setting up our cameras. Photography at this time did seem an intrusion on privacy; it was like photographing individuals absorbed in prayer in a village church—but this was a scene for which Gully Jimson would have sold everything but his artistic soul. It was the world coming to life, with all the noise mankind can make to gain the attention of the gods, and with all the colour a strong sun on a clear morning can conjure from earth and sky and flowing water and man-made things. Fifty years ago we could have reached for our sketch-pads and taken our places on the steps, but in these days of colour film we pranced about the ghats, changing lenses, stalking subjects, taking light readings and clicking our shutters in an orgy of photography; after a while the priests lost interest in us as bathers returned to collect their clothes and squatted around the platforms for the recitation of prayers.

About sixty beggars had taken up their positions for the day on steps leading to the Dasashwamedh ghat. Many of them were lepers and above the stubs of their fingers and toes the skin was scabrous and shiny. Dieter seemed to be well-informed about lepers and declared that if they went to hospital they would be treated without charge and could be cured.

'Go on to hospital, to HOSPITAL—Free treatment. Free treatment. You don't want to, huh? Because then you would have to work.' Dieter, who weighed about fourteen stone though he was less than average height, seemed to be shaken with indignation to the depths of his barrel-like body as he addressed the beggars, his expression a taunting grin, which elicited uncertain grins from the beggars.

'You see,' Dieter observed, 'when they have this disease they lose the hair above the eyes, and the skin of the arms and legs has a different colour. And you see that man without a nose? They have hereditary syphilis in this country, but usually they are resistant to it.'

He photographed a beggar sitting under a parasol in the centre of the steps: a dwarf whom the others seemed to have agreed to let sit in this favourable position. 'No photograph,' one beggar shouted at Hans, who impatiently waved him away. At this, the beggar with the rudimentary nose approached belligerently, snarling unintelligibly.

'Why are you shouting?' Hans growled. 'Get away,' and he pushed the man back.

It seemed an appallingly thoughtless thing to do. The beggar grabbed his stick and raised it. Hans prepared to strike him, and suddenly with shouts the other beggars bounded down the steps towards us sticks in hand.

The beggar nearest to me advanced purposefully and poked at me with a long bamboo but without much force, so I had no trouble catching it, and before any injury had been suffered by any of us, a tall man with greying hair, who was climbing the steps from the water, raised his hands and shouted at the beggars, ordering them to draw back. Out of the corner of my eye I saw Dieter take advantage of the lull that followed the stranger's command by leaping over a side wall, and a moment later Hans followed him, though he was less fortunate and received the end of a bamboo on his seat before he disappeared. My own assailant drew back and slowly all the beggars shuffled back to their places along the steps, our helper following them.

Boatmen now converged on us from the platform, assuring us that we could take excellent photographs from a boat without any interference, and so within a minute we were afloat and the ghats regained their beauty as the clamour subsided and only the high tinkle of a bell could be heard.

All too soon the boatman took us to the Jalsain Ghat, a short distance downstream and suggested that we view a cremation, adding a warning as we disembarked that we should not use our cameras lest they be snatched away from us.

The Jalsain ghat is the main cremation ghat of Benares and at any time during the day one is likely to see smoke rising from the funeral pyres near the water. A cremation was in progress, an economical one with only a small pile of wood logs that provided inadequate heat to consume the corpse with any speed. A thin elderly man stood nearby, phlegmatically stoking the fire from time to time.

Stretched out on the steps nearer the water was a very thin old woman with sunken jaws, who lay completely motionless save for the faintest of tremors that fluttered one cheek. As a guide standing nearby was quick to inform us she was waiting to die: after death she too would be cremated at Jalsain Ghat and her ashes would be cast upon the Ganges. Many a room in the mile-long complex of high buildings that border the ghats at Benares would be occupied by elderly people who had come to the city when they felt that death was imminent.

It was a relief to be out on the water again, but Benares still remained to be explored, and in the maze of alleys behind the ghats I enquired as discreetly as I could where the dancing girls of Benares, who I had been assured were famous, were to be found. When we came to the Chowk, the centre of the oldest quarter of the City we were approached by guides who wanted to take us to 'my sari factory' and 'my ivory factory', but learning where we wished to go they offered readily enough to take us to the Nautch (dance) girls, though it was obvious that they were rather puzzled by the request. They led the way to a street off the Chowk which was called the Dalmandi, a way lined with shops at street level, but differing from other streets in that above each shop was a curtained balcony. Behind the curtains one had glimpses of the women who were described to us as Benares' Nautch girls.

'You get dance girl alright', one of the two guides who seemed to be quarrelling about whose clients we were assured us, 'real dance girl', and he added in a whisper, 'most girls only for bed work'. The other guide drew our attention to individual girls. 'That is Bengali girl you see, and that one she is Nepali. Here there are girls from all over, Madrasis, Kashmiris, Punjabis, South Indian girls.'

Dieter for some reason became agitated and declared that it was time for lunch, adding that we could always come back, but Hans was impatient to see a dancing girl at once. After a hasty palaver in the cobbled street we followed one of the guides through a dark entrance into a murky little courtyard lit only by the thin light entering through a grille. Dieter now urged me to be extremely cautious against possible foul play because he had all his cash and camera equipment on him. When the guide took my hand to guide me up some steps in pitch darkness, Dieter barked that if hands were to be taken in the darkness then we should leave at once. His voice was harsh with mistrust. Slowly we mounted the steps and on emerging from the gloom came upon an old woman sitting at an oven making chuppattis by the side of the metal grille we had seen from below. Nothing could have looked more innocent. In the next room, which overlooked the street, five men argued with, and gave advice to, two young women, and when we appeared with the two guides bickering started regarding the price we should be asked to pay for seeing a dance. We were asked to pay in advance and this we refused to do, but eventually, having removed our shoes, we were permitted to cross the threshold of the door into a dim room where the curtains were drawn tight across the balcony. The floor was thickly carpeted, and against one wall were three fat bolsters on which we were invited to seat ourselves. A scratch band appeared and the musicians ranged themselves by us; a tabla man, a harmonium player and a one-eyed man with a strange instrument called a dilruba, which was about two feet long with wires and cross-pieces that made it look like a species of beetle. Meanwhile, in a coy flurry in one corner, the young lady who was our Nautch girl changed her sari, screened by the second woman and a surly-looking man holding a baby. The girl had a fresh, open face, and lovely teeth. When she was dressed, she squatted in front of us and asked very engagingly for the money in advance, but however reluctant a low-budget traveller is to talk about money with a lady, he is even more reluctant to part with it without some assurance of getting value for it, and so we haggled, she and I, and finally it was agreed that we give half in advance and half when we left. As it became obvious that no-one intended to steal our cameras and that the entertainers were more apprehensive of us than we were of them, we relaxed and nodded genially as the band scraped their instruments. I do not know what we expected; something breathtaking perhaps, after the furtive approach and the conspiratorial whisperings in the corner.

The girl tied a string of bells round each ankle; the dilruba player, whose one eye seemed to be privy to all human lust and folly, scraped his instrument; the harmonium player, whose mouth was coloured red with pan juice, poked at the keys with spurious enthusiasm and the tabla man thumped away, eyeing our cameras appraisingly the while. The girl was delightful, dancing with the self-consciousness of a five-year-old who had just learnt the first steps; here was no magic at all, nothing exotic, nothing suggestive, though the band tried to generate an excitement that was entirely absent by simulating some passion in their playing. The dance was soon over and the money paid, and three innocents abroad took their leave, their curiosity satisfied, quite prepared to overlook their dancer's obvious incompetence, rejecting the guides' assurance that dancing was for this girl, as for most of the girls in the street, a cover only.

In the Chowk area the streets are narrow and congested and perhaps this is the Benares that struck Kim as 'a peculiarly filthy city', but now, though it must be crowded as it ever was, the Chowk is not notably filthy. As I wandered through the lanes in the afternoon I was enthralled by all the life and colour and more than once was pushed out of danger by the passenger of a cycle-rickshaw as I gazed about me, unaware for the moment of the impatient traffic: there, swaggering along, came two Baluchi money-lenders, from far in the north-west of the subcontinent, staffs in their hands, embroidered waistcoats over their loose shirts, off to collect their interest; there came a cycle-rickshaw carrying a corpse wrapped in white and tied with rope between two bamboo poles, the man in attendance sitting nonchalantly as any passenger; here was a square nearly lost from sight off the Chowk, its concrete surface radiant with the dazzling gold of piles of marigolds; there was a sign outside a dentist's shop depicting great grinning false teeth, and beyond it was a shrine set under a peepul tree; wherever I looked there was something curious to hold my attention. In all the main lanes where tourists were likely to pass eager youngsters offered to act as guides, or claimed to be the owners of factories where especially cheap rates were offered: these were some of the intelligent unemployed, masters of instant familiarity and friendliness whose brown eyes became resentful if one did not heed them.

'I am not a guide', one would disclaim hotly, or 'I am not a commission man'. They roamed the alleys to draw prospective buyers to a particular shop where they would receive a commission on purchases. Shopkeepers themselves, once they were sure of a customer, tried to avoid paying commission by warning the tourist not to listen to such opportunists in future. If one wanted a good intelligence service in Benares, one could not do better than engage the city's commission men, greyhounds of men who were aware of the wanderings of all visitors. One of them told me something about himself.

'I tell you very frankly, I am a commission agent. I get five per cent. Some people will tell you they are students and you should avoid them. I think I will go to Bombay where the opportunities of meeting tourists are greater. I have a contact in the Taj Mahal Hotel, a receptionist. Here one has not the opportunities; the rich tourists stay in the hotels in the Cantonment, and those hotels own fifty per cent of the silk trade in Benares. When the tourists want information they contact the tourist office, and the guides there, who have a retainer from the hotel people, conduct the tourists to the factories of the hoteliers which means that the tourists are not free for the whole market, and it makes it very difficult for us to contact them.'

Most of the Benares silk is woven by Muslims, lean, bearded men who work in 'factories' off the main ways at the centre of the city, at wooden looms that use a system of punched cards for changing the patterns. Sometimes three or four looms are housed in one room, one man and perhaps a boy apprentice handling each loom. The weavers I saw seemed surprised that anyone should be interested in their work, yet they produced saris and other silk work so brilliant in colour and design that even in the murk of the 'factories', their beauty could be seen.

The bazaar where the silk is sold is called the Rani Kuan Chowk. Here the shops are open late, and little interest seems to be taken in business or anything else in the mornings, but after dark the bazaar becomes a treasure house of shimmering colours. The buyers sit in their stalls, some three or four feet above the level of the street, lords of the night to whom the weavers bring the saris produced during the day, each sari wrapped in tissue paper and packed in a cardboard carton. When the saris are released from the cartons cataracts of silk gleam in the light, sari over sari as the sellers strive for a sale, while the buyers look on inscrutably, all the power of disposition in their cold eyes. Benares is noted for its fine silk and saris, and no tourist could fail to be aware of this, if only because of the remarkable advertising of one firm of silk merchants whose slogan is painted in huge letters on the walls and pavements of the city, and even on the buildings over the ghats: 'King of Baranasi sarees, Choudhury Brothers, Thatheri Bazar.'

Thatheri bazaar is really the bazaar of the sellers of brass and copper wares but the stalls of the dealers in silk overlap from the Rani Kuan Chowk. The best time to come here is around noon, the only time that the sun penetrates the narrow paved way, for then the metal pots and the various metal household goods and ornamental palanquins that line the front of each stall gleam dazzlingly in the light.

Leading into Thatheri bazaar is Kachuri Galli (Kachuri being a species of puri, a light puffy ball made from batter and eaten with curry), where the stalls of the sellers of incense sticks, who also stock mildly erotic literature, are succeeded by the kitchens of the Kachuri-wallahs and the halwais (sweetsellers) who cater not so much for the pilgrims as for the permanent inhabitants of the city, the priests and shopkeepers and those who provide services along the ghats. I met a bizarre trio in this galli: they looked dehydrated, with bright powdery make-up and attenuated bodies, and eyes like flames in their powdered sockets.

'You take our photos?' one of them croaked in a flat voice, too deep for a woman, and I backed away explaining that the light was bad.

'Neuters', growled a shopkeeper in a nearby stall, 'dancers'.

Sometimes part of the life that flows along the Chowk swirls through these bazaars and distracts the stallholders for a moment from their business. Sometimes one would meet a number of Marwari women walking in procession through the alleys, chanting as they took a newly-wedded couple to the temple to be blessed. Another chant portended something quite different, for on hearing it one could expect to see four men carrying a corpse bound to poles above their heads, their destination the burning ghat. More affluent funeral processions kept to the Chowk, where one might see a corpse borne on a truck decorated with banked marigolds and followed by a chanting procession. Benares, dealing as it does in blessings and the forgiveness of sins, is never still.

Sarnath, four miles north of Benares, where the Lord Buddha preached his first sermon, was once a city of note, as the Chinese pilgrims Fa Hian and Hiuen Tsang, who visited Sarnath in the fifth and seventh centuries respectively, testified. Today there is little to see on the silent plain except the Dhamek Stupa, built in the Gupta period. The Sarnath Museum, however, has an exhibit of outstanding interest, the capital of Ashoka's pillar, the symbol of today's Indian Union.

Near the Dhamek Stupa is a Jain temple, the original perhaps of the Temple of Tirthankers where Kim's lama stayed with kindly monks between his journeys in search of the River of Healing. Sarnath is sacred to the Jains because one of their Tirthankers ('Path-makers', guides to Nirvana) attained perfection in the neighbourhood.

For the five days that I was in Benares I stayed at the Benares Tourist Bungalow near the cantonments, which proved to be one of the popular halting places of the world's hippies and other low-budget travellers.

Twelve people, including Hans, Dieter and myself, shared a dormitory. The other dormitory residents included two young Frenchmen who dressed in dhothis and wandered about barefooted; a taciturn New Zealander who looked as if he had just returned from two months in the bush; a spruce Dutchman with a beard and moustache similar to those of the Laughing Cavalier, who had, however, forgotten how to smile, let alone laugh; a Swede, tall, slim and bearded who had had the fortune to meet and team up with a Norwegian girl along the way; an American with the gaunt appearance of a man who had ridden the ranges in all weathers; and a stocky fellow with golden hair and beard who slept in the next bed to mine and seemed to have no other possessions than a cake of soap, a boater hat with a marigold in it, and a mongrel dog that slept under his bed.

Few of these travellers had enough money to insulate themselves from the pressures of crowd life and the constant scrabble for mere existence in India, and their nerves and tempers had suffered during their travels through the country. Dieter, who seemed relatively well-off, told me how he had dealt with Indians who shoved him in the trains.

'I hit them,' he explained. 'When I was coming here, I come a long distance, ja, and I am sitting near the window, ja, and suddenly, right under my nose appears a big brown foot through the window, so I twist it, yes, and then I close the window on it.' I was sceptical about some of his stories of this kind, but the sentiments appeared to find approval among the other travellers staying in the dormitory.

As to Hans, I had seen how he reacted to the beggars and had also witnessed his handling of a cycle-rickshaw wallah. On one occasion when he had been with me he had asked the fare to somewhere close by and was automatically told 'One rupee'.

'One rupee?' he repeated.

'Hah sahib, one rupee.'

'Good. I have your rickshaw for one rupee?'

'Hah sahib.'

Hans handed over one rupee and pretended to walk off with the rickshaw, looking very grim and resolute as he did so. His attitude in general to fare demands was: 'I don't listen to what they say. When they take me where I want to go, I give them what I think.'

The Swede had spent two months in India. 'I fight them here on the trains for a place,' he declared. 'They spread everywhere, lie on the floor. The other day, I ask one man to move and he don't so I catch him and shake him till he cry.'

It seemed to me that at this low-budget level, travel was causing a good deal of mutual loathing between foreigners and Indians and was not quite 'the better understanding between our countries' that idealists suppose travel to create.

The ones who appeared to derive the greatest pleasure from their travels were the two Frenchmen who were making the most of the company of the occasional female travellers staying at the bungalow, and who had developed a lucrative business selling student cards to other travellers.

'Who is paying full fare on the railways?' one would ask. Someone would nod sleepily. 'Aha, why have you no student card? You are not a student? Well that is not the thing; I can give you a student card. You see, here is a blank card, all official, showing that the holder is a student and registered with the International Students' Federation in Holland. I have two hundred of them. I fill it in for you, stamp your photograph with an official stamp and you give me ten rupees. With my student card it cost me only ten rupees to travel from Delhi to here. Ten rupees: usually I don't pay. When the ticket collector asks me for a ticket, I shout "Ticket? Ticket?" and I act so'—he waved his arms about and looked like a lunatic—'but for ten rupees—yes it is easier to pay.'

13

Travelling east from Benares along the Grand Trunk Road I would soon enter Bihar, a state little known in the west though it did acquire notoriety during the famine of the mid-1960s. The northern part of the state lies in the Ganges plain and for most of its way through Bihar the Grand Trunk Road would be passing across the plain, south of the Ganges.

The route would not take me through any famous cities: Bihar has no cities that are likely to be well known outside India, though Patna, the state capital, has given its name to Patna rice. The city of Gaya, south of the Ganges, is held by Hindus to be of great sanctity. Neighbouring Buddh Gaya, though little more than a village, is famous among Buddhists as the place where the Buddha received enlightenment. I hoped to visit Buddh Gaya, which will doubtless be developed in time to encourage visitors from such countries as Japan.

Many states in India are making a considerable effort to attract Indian tourists from other states, and produce a great deal of tourist literature and general tracts on their regions. If Bihar too is doing this it is having little impact, for even in neighbouring Uttar Pradesh few people seemed to know anything about Bihar, except to say it was 'backward'. In Allahabad a university lecturer had described Biharis to me as being 'cunning', and that too was how my neighbour on the bus from Benares described them.

Bihar deserves to have a much better public relations system than it has.

The bus I boarded at Benares belonged to Bihar and had no bell connection between the conductor and driver, a characteristic of Bihari buses I was to find. When the conductor wanted the driver to stop he would bang on the side of the bus, or shout, either of which was alarming and especially so when the driver turned round to look at the conductor while the bus was still travelling at full speed.

Ten miles east of Benares is Moghulserai, a major railway junction that acquired notoriety after the murder there in 1968 of Deen Dayal Upadhyaya, leader of the Jan Sangh, which was, after the Congress party, the most powerful political group in India. His body had been found near the tracks at Moghulserai railway station and subsequent investigations lasted for months. Questions were asked in parliament, speculation kept the press well supplied with articles that maintained public interest. The setting for the murder, the character of the dead man and his political status, the fact that his death could be construed as a very welcome event for some politicians . . . all the circumstances had strong dramatic possibilities. After months of investigations the police statement came as an anti-climax: the victim had been murdered, they said, by a thief, murdered for the contents of his bedroll.

Sasaram, in Bihar, is seventy-three miles from Benares, and I spent a feverish night there at the PWD resthouse in company with a good proportion of the town's mosquito population. But though I slept indifferently that night, it happened as the psalmist has said: 'Heaviness may endure for a night but joy cometh in the morning' (*Psalms* 30, 5), and I awoke free of the fever, and fit for the road again.

The red stone mausoleum of Sher Shah Suri on the outskirts of Sasaram is an impressive monument to the man who laid the foundations of the modern Grand Trunk Road, and has what the caretaker claimed is the second highest dome in India, one hundred and one feet from the floor to the apex. I thought that was all there was to see in Sasaram. Then when I set out again I saw a helmeted policeman and a goat on point duty at the crossroads near the station. The goat stood with its front feet on the policeman's tunic while he, directing traffic the while, fed it bananas. The affable policeman stopped a truck for me and I was installed with some cases of machinery and taken twelve miles on to Dehri-on-Son by the west bank of the Son River.

It was pretty countryside. Small fields were dotted with trees and ricks of rice-straw raised on stilts, and the farmhouses were neat little red-tiled cottages. We passed many bullock-carts laden with household furniture and topped by a bed or charpai, the legs of the beds being decoratively carved and painted, and we were passed by two cars, each with a bed tied to its roof. The truck-driver explained that this was one of the periods of the year ordained by pundits as being auspicious for the celebration of marriages and these bullock-carts were taking the brides' dowries to their husbands' homes.

The Son is crossed by the longest bridge in India, nearly two miles long. It appears, to the man on foot, even longer than its 10,000 feet or so, but I was spared the walk because I hitched a ride on a bullock-cart and crossed in comfort reading the headlines in the *Statesman*. Then, this being my day, a truck stopped without my having flagged it. The Punjabi driver had started that morning from Mirzapur, between Allahabad and Benares and intended to reach Calcutta, 330 miles from where we were, before midnight. We stopped after a few miles by a couple of flimsy shelters set in a broad, dusty clearing, a Grand Trunk Road transport café, where a dozen trucks were already parked in the shadiest places, with their bonnets raised while their crews either dozed on charpais or drank tea. The owner or manager of the café was a skinny Sikh with discoloured teeth, eyes flecked with yellow and a face twisted by a hideous scar down his forehead. One of the drivers had only one eye and when he drank half a glass of '3X' rum the other drivers joked that whereas before he could see only half of the road he would now see nothing. They were a tough-looking group, these drivers, and they needed to be tough driving in India, for they faced worse hazards than bad roads. A Swiss missionary doctor whom I had met in Benares had told me about a recent incident near Jubbalpore, where a child had run in front of a truck and been run over. The driver had promptly run away, but his mate, whose job was merely to give signals, had been too slow: the villagers had dragged him from the cab and lynched him. That drivers expected summary punishment was evident from the number of newspaper reports about accidents that concluded: 'The driver escaped, leaving the vehicle on the spot', 'The jeep escaped' or the truck-driver escaped'. That the drivers were wise to flee was evident from newspaper reports like the following:

> 'THREE KNOCKED DOWN AND INJURED BY BUS
>
> Dum Dum—Three people were knocked down and injured by a Calcutta-bound private bus at Ghughudanga on the Dum Dum Road on Saturday night. After the accident, an angry crowd stopped the vehicle and manhandled its driver. A police party, arriving at the spot, foiled attempts to damage the bus. The injured were taken to a Calcutta hospital. The driver was arrested.

After the incident, panic-striken drivers of other buses, plying between Shyambazar and Dum Dum airport, diverted their vehicles from the area, causing inconvenience to passengers for some time.'

On the way again, a few miles beyond the café, both the driver and his mate pointed out a large village and shook their heads significantly:

'Thieves,' said the driver. The people in this village were not to be trusted at night, he said, and neither for that matter were the people who lived near the café. 'If a truck is going slow near these places, the people will leap onto the back and loot.' The worst stretch for robbers, he said, began ten miles beyond nearby Shergatti and continued through fourteen miles of hills where trucks had to travel in low gear. No truck would travel singly along this stretch between 10 pm and 3 am but only in convoy, with the front trucks bearing loads and the last truck carrying half a dozen men with lathis (staves) as a precaution against robbers.

'But surely the police must know about the thieves,' I suggested. They laughed. 'The police are in league with them. The Bihar police are no good.'

Shergatti, the place they had mentioned, is fifty-seven miles from Sasaram, and I alighted there for Gaya, twenty miles to the north. Gaya is not quite so holy to the Hindus as Benares, but still a place of great sanctity. I found it unattractive, dirty and overcrowded. A common habit of children in an old quarter of the town was to sit on the verandah in front of their houses and defecate over the edge into the street or drain. The most remarkable thing I saw in Gaya was a completely naked man, a sturdy fellow, marching along one of the main roads with his hefty genitalia striking his thighs at every stride: he had ash marks on his forehead and I gathered that he was a holy man.

Buddh Gaya, seven miles to the south east of Gaya, is the centre of the Buddhist Universe, and a tall shrine—the Vihara—stands near the spot where Buddhists believe that the Buddha attained Enlightenment. It is the most venerated of Buddhist shrines but oddly enough does not technically belong to the Buddhists. In fact, for years it was held to belong to a local Hindu sect, and it was only after the Buddh Gaya Temple Act of 1949 was passed, appointing a committee to manage the temple, comprised of four Hindus and four Buddhists, with the District Magistrate of Gaya as ex-officio chairman, that the Buddhists had any control over it.

The original cause of this situation was the destruction of Buddh Gaya by Muslim invaders in the early thirteenth century, until which time it had been controlled by Buddhists. No record seems to have survived about Buddh Gaya in the next three-and-a-half centuries but it is supposed that the monks fled during the period of the Muslim invasion and that Buddh Gaya then reverted to the jungle. A wandering Sanyasi monk discovered the shrine at the end of the sixteenth century and, impressed by the woods and silence, decided to settle there. He founded a monastery, which eventually grew so powerful that by the time the zamindari (landlord) system was abolished after Independence, the Mahant, the chief monk of the monastery in whom the property was invested, was the second biggest landlord in Bihar. Early Mahants had come to consider the temple and its surrounds as their own property and they continued to control it even after it was rebuilt as the result of Buddhist efforts in the nineteenth century, because the Buddha is considered by Hindus to be the ninth incarnation of the god Vishnu.

The fixed population of Buddh Gaya is predominantly Hindu, but for the greater part of the year numbers of Buddhist pilgrims live in various monasteries and guesthouses near the Vihara, and these pilgrims and monks provide the greater part of the interest, colour and charm of the place—the stocky Burmese monks in yellow robes; the slender Laotian monks in orange; the red-robed Tibetan monks, giants in the plains of India, with wind-cured leather faces, and eyes like shuttered moons, slow-moving and quick to smile, absorbed for most of the day in prayers and meditation.

The Vihara is on a hillock and dominates Buddh Gaya. A bazaar at the foot of the hillock extends for some way along the road to Gaya and where the bazaar ends the Sanyasi Math (monastery) starts, its gate adjoining the shack of a spry little man who claimed to be seventy-five, bullied his wife, and sold the best curds in the bazaar. The Math was built when memories of invasion were still fresh and is like a fort. The way from the entrance gate, once stoutly barred, passes between two high walls, and abuts on a flagged courtyard that even today has a medieval appearance, with stables for horses and elephants, a broad well and a thick defensive inner wall guarding the heart of the monastery. The present Mahant possesses one elephant, a great old bull with filed tusks bound with

15 The Grand Trunk Road in Uttar Pradesh

16 Cycle rickshaws in Bihar

17 Benares dentist

18 Bus transit

silver, which is usually tethered in the yard and taken out on ceremonial occasions when the Mahant rides in procession. The monastery has a forbidding air but the Mahant is very accessible, to visitors as well as locals.

The Burmese monastery, opposite the Mahant's mango groves, is the last building in Buddh Gaya on the road to Gaya and it was here that I was given a bed by the genial young Burmese monk who was in sole charge while his superior was in Burma raising funds to maintain the place. Two young Englishmen and a tall, improbable-looking character in dark glasses, sequined skull cap and yellow robes like those worn by the monks, were already living there. All three were rather taciturn and elusive and I had been at the monastery for two days before I discovered that the tall fellow in dark glasses was no monk but an American hippy. They were all studying meditation and went each morning to a nearby ashram founded by Vinobhe Bhave. All were still in their first phase of enthusiasm and self-discipline, so I would find them sitting in dark corners staring unblinking at spots on the wall, or pacing the flat roof of the monastery, passing round and round the unrailed perimeter, trying to concentrate, though had any one of them achieved the state he strove for he would certainly have fallen over the edge.

After a first night indoors, when I was troubled by mosquitoes, I pulled my charpai onto the roof, at a lower level than the roof on which the meditators walked. On my second night, when I had stripped down to my underpants and was rubbing myself with mosquito repellent, I happened to see a movement above and saw what looked like long, blonde hair moving in the breeze as someone walked round on the main roof. It seemed a very odd and a stirring sight to see in a Buddhist monastery. A short while later it appeared again, long, blonde hair, and a moment later a brunette passed, a statuesque girl, unmistakably European in the clear starlight, though she wore Indian dress. It transpired that the two girls were also staying at the monastery and studying meditation; the blonde girl was American, the brunette Greek, and they must have provided a stern test for those others striving to concentrate and to ignore the flesh.

Life in Buddh Gaya was very tranquil. I would wake at dawn to the stentorian voice of the monk in charge of the Mahant's mango grove, an old man who wore steel-rimmed spectacles tied to his ears with string. Every morning he collected a small fee from those who came to the grove each day to take away fallen mango leaves in tall wicker baskets, the leaves being mixed with dung to make fuel. One morning I awakened to see the Mahant's elephant passing by little more than a trunk's length away.

I would take a short-cut through the fields to a tented restaurant outside the Tibetan monastery, run by a charming elderly Tibetan couple who came to Buddh Gaya each winter from Manali in the Kulu Valley. Only two dishes were served here, but they were cheap and nourishing and I did not tire of them. One was 'Mormors', balls of chopped onions and meat cased in a suet crust; the other was 'Thoopa', a soupy mixture of noodles and a morsel of mince sprinkled with paprika; and one ate Tibetan bread, dark brown and leathery and shaped like a buckle, with both.

I came to distinguish some of the characters of Buddh Gaya. One of the friendliest Tibetans was a one-legged monk who hopped about very nimbly with the aid of a crutch and like the other Tibetans emanated an aura of physical strength and patience. He welcomed visitors to the Tibetan temple in the monastery, and it was he who usually sat in the room where pilgrims came to turn a gigantic prayer wheel, and gently pointed out their error to those barbarians who would turn the wheel anticlockwise, explaining that those who would achieve grace must always walk round any hallowed object in a clockwise direction. I do not know what the Tibetans made of the local population of pygmies, who were ever arguing and shouting. The locals liked the Tibetans well enough; they were generous, gentle and child-like, lacking in guile. The beggar children from surrounding villages approached the Tibetans with complete confidence and held their hands. One little beggar boy was called 'Langra', 'the lame one', and he made dramatic use of his crutch. A little beggar girl led by the hand another girl, who walked as if in a trance and showed only the whites of her eyes. These three were very tenacious and during my first two days in Buddh Gaya they croaked after me, plucking my shirt whenever I was anywhere near the temple. Later, however, realizing I was no rich 'Ungraij', and that I understood their talk, they would greet me unprofessionally, the crippled boy nimble enough without his crutch, the two girls chattering unguardedly with bright eyes.

I had made friends with the old Sanyasi monk who shouted in the mango grove every morning, but some of his fellows at the monastery were not quite so charming. In an enclosure within the monastery walls were a number of shrines and when I visited these a resident priest pointed out large footprints in stone. 'Buddha', he claimed. 'Visitors . . .' he continued, pausing as he drew a handful of rupee notes from his pockets, 'Visitors pay two, three rupees for Buddha puja'. (Puja is a ritual offering.) He snorted when I ignored the hint, and when I remarked that if money was always charged poor people would not be able to attend the temple and have prayers said for them, he left me in disgust, saying that in that case I could look around alone, for visitors normally gave him two rupees; the gulf between the sharp and the simple in India is very wide indeed. As I was leaving the monastery a monk followed me and tried to sell me for four rupees what he claimed was an old Nepali coin.

The three most obvious 'characters' in Buddh Gaya were all slightly mad. One of them, a sprite of a man, a feckless Ariel, flitted around in the Mahant's mango grove all day, and whenever he saw me he would run out into the road behind me blowing a whistle and then wait, standing to attention in the middle of the road, a forlorn figure, incoherent and shy yet at such moments eager for company. He wore a postman's cap and a khaki shirt and shorts, and seemed to have some military experience, for he would stamp his skinny legs and a wire-like arm would come to the salute as I came to chat with him. On his shirt pocket he wore a German hair-clip and a Marmite label as though they were medals, and in his pocket he always carried a visiting card that had once belonged to a factory manager from Ludhiana. Whenever I left him I felt that I was deserting a young child, for the light would die in his eyes and he would shuffle back disconsolately into the mango grove. He loved to talk to the visitors at the Burmese dharamsala. An Englishman who had recently left had tended a suppurating wound on his leg and Tom the American was now giving him ointment when it was necessary. The poor man did not have India's substitute for National Health, a family to look after him, and I had a notion that he had wandered far from his home.

The second of Buddh Gaya's deranged inhabitants was a burly man with an expression of great ferocity, who wore a sheepskin jacket and a close-fitting skin cap even in the mid-day heat, and looked like one who has almost seen the truth and had it stolen from him. Each day he was to be seen in the same quarter of the bazaar, striding up and down along the dusty verge of the road, scowling and muttering to himself. Local shopkeepers fed him. The third 'character' was a woman who sat in the bazaar chiding shoppers or passing the time by beating a pot lid with a stick.

The Burmese monastery was bordered on one side by wheatfields. Water hereabouts lay some twelve feet below the surface of the ground and the common way of drawing it was by using a shadoof—an upright pole near the wellhead, with a second pole, fitted at one end with a bucket and at the other with a stone, fastened to it in such a way that it could pivot. The empty bucket would be let down the well and drawn up when full with the aid of the stone counter-balance. The local men were hard workers and they were busy at the shadoofs all day, pouring water from the buckets into the irrigation channels; they were friendly and hospitable and though they were short in stature they looked strong. Their womenfolk also worked hard, and at this time they were harvesting pulses and carrying the plants to the villages; when they were not in the fields they sat in the shade by their houses delousing one another's hair.

The inhabitants of the village that lay a couple of hundred yards over the fields from the Burmese monastery were labourers who lived in mud huts set in a picturesque ring of palm trees which they tapped for toddy. They had few memories of the Bihar famine. The last wheat crop had been bad, but the winter crop of rice had been fair. Rice was planted in July each year and harvested in the last week of December and the first week of January.

The next village, half a mile away, belonged to Brahmans. Here the houses were made of stone and the farmers hired men from the neighbouring village as labourers. Some of these farmers had tube-wells on their properties, and I was intrigued to see that the boys sometimes carried the keys to the tube-well sheds tied to the end of their Brahmanical cords, which were worn over the left shoulder and under the right arm. During a discussion with some of the men of this village I asked what the minimum age now was for marriage. A boy of thirteen was pointed out to me and I was told that he had been married for two years. Was there not a law now, I asked, relating to the minimum age permitted for marriage? A number of men started to answer me heatedly, and then an elder said with some irritation that governments rely on people, not people on governments, and that the people of the village would continue to do as they pleased and marry their children young. I said I was delighted by such independence of mind and asked why it was considered necessary to marry children when they were so young, but they would not answer this beyond saying that it was their custom.

Tom, the American, was no zombie or ascetic and was enjoying life in Buddh Gaya. Like the other meditators he paid nothing to the guru at the ashram, and accommodation at the monastery was free. He reckoned he could live on little more than two rupees a day, about eighty-five dollars a year; meditation was a convenient way by which he could defer the day when he would have to return home and earn enough money for another trip abroad. Tom was a great talker; he was well-read and well-travelled and had a deep fund of esoteric knowledge. He would quote from books that appear in few public libraries, and seemed to know much about such people as those who smuggle pornography from Sweden to the Arab countries and those who smuggle hashish from Chitral to the West. He had a note-book full of information gleaned from years of cheap travelling, of addresses in Europe and the East where one could obtain free accommodation, of airlines which sold cut-price tickets in contravention of IATA regulations; and many other notes of this kind. He possessed very little apart from this note-book, nothing more than would fit into a small rucksack: a luxurious sleeping bag which he said had cost US $100, an embroidered Afghan jacket, climbing boots in which he had trekked in Nepal, a spare shirt, underwear, toilet gear and a large pipe. That was all, and when he heard that I had lost my own pipe, he insisted that I take his, claiming that he had no use for it: 'It looks a bit dirty but it'll clean out. I smoked shit in it in Afghanistan.'

The Greek girl looked like a queen in Buddh Gaya, tall and slender and restless. Like Tom she called herself a hippy and when these two conversed their talk was barely intelligible, being mainly the relation of experiences of smoking 'shit'—gunja. The Burmese monk would listen to them benignly, sipping some beverage that he prepared himself and smoking American cigarettes. The American girl rarely spoke but looked out at the world with large blue eyes, an irrepressible smile on her full, and rather predatory, lips. The two young Englishmen talked about poetry and 'varsity' and, less self-consciously, about their adventures en route to India. On my second evening at the monastery we were joined by a Swiss traveller, the man who had been my neighbour in the dormitory at Benares, he who had kept a dog under his bed. He arrived in a two-horse-power Renault, his dog in the front seat, the rear seat piled with baggage, on his way to visit Darjeeling. His final plan was to go to Kathmandu, sell his car—thereby, he hoped, making his fortune—then go to Japan in the hope that he would be able to work there as an architect. The dog, he said, had been very useful to him when he drove alone through the East but he had not acquired it as a watchdog. I had joined him in Hungary, because the girl who had then been travelling with him had liked dogs and he had kept the animal, a friendly, hairy mongrel, after the girl had left him.

14

The old monk's strong voice from across the road in the mango grove woke me as usual on my last morning in Buddh Gaya, calm and beautiful Buddh Gaya, and it was with regret that I set out again on my way. Rather to my surprise I discovered that the freemasonry of cycle-rickshaw wallahs was as strong in Buddh Gaya as it had been at nearly every stage on my route; no-one was prepared to lose his honour by charging me the correct fare, eight annas, for the two-mile journey to a main way where I hoped to catch an early bus that would take me to the Grand Trunk Road.

That evening I reached Nimiaghat, one hundred and one miles on at the foot of Parasnath mountain, on the top of which, tradition has it, the twenty-third Tirthanker of the Jains is buried. It had been a long day of walking, interspersed with bus and truck rides.

The following day found me another fifty miles on, just inside the Bengal border. I had passed through a green, rolling landscape for most of the two days, through country where rice had displaced wheat as the main crop. Outside every village stood stacks of rice-straw on platforms built on stilts so that water would drain away after rain. Bamboo proliferated in this region and was used as a base for thatch on roofs and also for making screens that gave some degree of privacy to the local houses. The cutting and carrying of the bamboo appeared to be a feminine preserve and it was common to see women tripping across the Grand Trunk Road carrying bundles of bamboo on their heads. Beyond the Parasnath hills the landscape flattened again and the first signs of industrialization became apparent; for the rest of the way to Calcutta the horizon was rarely free of factory smoke.

I was intrigued by a number of diggings beside the road, most of them triangular hollows about a foot deep. The earth had been taken from these hollows to level the verges of the road, and the diggings were this shape so that it was easy to calculate the work done by and the remuneration due to each worker.

At Topchanchi, eight miles from Nimiaghat, was a Bihar state government check-post, set up to ensure that tax was paid on all dutiable goods entering the State; the price of rice, for instance, varied between Bihar and Bengal, and rice could not be carried freely between the states. An officer at the check-post talked enthusiastically about India and then admitted that he had never in his life been to Bengal, though its boundary was only forty miles away. He was helpful and after I had drunk tea with him, arranged a lift for me on a truck driven by Punjabis. And so I came to the Bengal border sitting on the roof of the cab in company with a young Sikh, who called himself the 'conductor' of the truck.

I was the only passenger until we were out of sight of the check-post but then we stopped and men who had been squatting by the road swarmed up the ropes to sit atop the tall load: the truck crew were making some pocket money, charging the regular bus fare to returning holiday-makers. Now I understood why the Sikh called himself the conductor; this was his function on the roof, marshalling the passengers and collecting their money. Officially such a service would not be encouraged and that was why the passengers dismounted whenever the truck approached a check-post and walked on for about a mile, to rejoin the truck after it had been cleared.

The young Sikh was proud and happy in his work and maintained that trucking was the best-paid occupation in India. The driver, he said, received 150 rupees basic pay and 150 rupees 'fooding allowance' per month; the co-driver received Rs 125 basic, plus Rs 150 'fooding allowance' per month; and he himself received Rs 60 basic and Rs 120 'fooding allowance'. This money was augmented by what they could make carrying passengers. He said that he sent his basic pay back home each month and spent the remainder on food. He was only nineteen years old, but had already worked for six years on the truck and had travelled as far as the 'fine, clean city' of Bombay, where he maintained one could 'get a woman for just two rupees'. It was a great life, he assured me, he had loved every moment of it and his eyes gleamed at the recollection of what he had seen during years on the road.

I alighted at Chirkunda, in the heart of the industrial complex of the government-owned Damodar Valley Corporation, where wages were high, prices proportionately higher and men lived in the midst of rusting metal and grinding machine parts. This was still the heart of the coal belt, but water power was also being harnessed and fed into the factories of the area. The Damodar and Barakar rivers both

19 The Vihara at Buddh Gaya

20 The author on an elephant at Buddh Gaya

21 Sanyasi monks at Buddh Gaya

22 Bazaar in Buddh Gaya

23 Common form of irrigation in Bihar—the shadoof

24 A Persian water wheel

provide hydro-electric power. I stayed the night by the Barakar river, the boundary between Bihar and Bengal, at Maithon, the site of a barrage and hydro-electric station. On one side of the river lay as doleful a collection of dead or dying heavy machinery as I have ever seen anywhere, with moribund-looking people to match; but the other bank was so cleverly landscaped that one was unaware of the industrial belt over the water. The government had built a guest-house on a little island in the lake formed by the barrage, a delightful place reached by a bridge, and there I was given a single room with windows on three sides overlooking the lake, and a private bathroom, for a charge of Rs 2 a night. Across a narrow strait was a yacht club for Europeans working on various projects in the area, and beyond that was a little cove where rowing boats could be hired and where the paddle steamer that operated for short pleasure trips on the lake was berthed. This thirty-foot paddle steamer, the *Mallard,* had once belonged to the Maharajah of Patiala and perhaps it had once carried distinguished guests on the lake in the grounds of the Moti Bagh Palace in Patiala. It was a long way from the regal Moti Bagh to a barrage on the border of West Bengal, from a Maharajah's company to parties of day trippers. The *Mallard* still had a day of glory before her, however, for, together with other craft of the Maharajah's flotilla, she had been bought after Partition by the Damodar Valley Corporation and Pandit Nehru had sat in one of her little leather armchairs in the bow, and taken a pleasure trip on the lake after he had officially opened the Maithon Dam in 1957.

A column had been erected near the dam 'In memory of those who laid down their lives in the construction of this project', a memorial to simple people with little notion of mechanics or electricity, workers like those one sees at every building site in India among the bricks or on ladders or up the crazy bamboo scaffolding, with baskets of sand or earth or bricks upon their heads; men, women and children with little idea of safety and few protective aids, who in the days when the dam was being built had only a vague idea of what they were achieving, but were beginning nevertheless to conceive the idea that what was being built was their own. Many of the massive projects completed in those first exciting years have had sorry records since they were proudly opened and 'dedicated to the people of India', but it is a matter for pride that they were built at all. Many people I conversed with considered that India had given premature attention to her industries, that she should have started with education and agriculture, and phased in industrialization more gradually; but India has governed herself for only a quarter of a century in modern times, and has accomplished much even if she has learnt only her priorities.

Next morning, puppies were rolling about playing on the verandah, while their mother, sleek-coated and content, lay in the first warmth of the sun. I could see from my windows the paddle steamer rounding the spit on the island with an early load of trippers, and the yachts in the little yacht club basin reflected the sunlight. In my room a little lizard gripped the wall, its eyes bulging and agitated; I had seen it fall off earlier, and it had lain askew on my wooden bed, panting, its translucent skin working like bellows, but after a minute it had scurried away unharmed and resumed its stance on the wall.

It was a restful place and its charm derived partly from the manager and from my fellow guests; all had the air of wayfarers who have found a haven and know how to rest. The manager, who had been batman to an RAF officer during the war and spoke English, lived in a cottage adjoining the guesthouse with his wife, four sons, two daughters, a dog, seven puppies, three goats and a cow and appeared to be a man who had come to terms very successfully with life. For once I was reluctant to be upon my way in the morning.

Maithon had proved so pleasant a surprise that I became enthusiastic at the prospect of visiting the great steel mills at Durgapur, forty miles further along the Grand Trunk Road. When I reached there, however, I found the town of Durgapur a dreary place, and wasted so much time finding accommodation that I never reached the steel mills. What impressed me most about the place was the philosophy of the students at a local school who had recently demonstrated because they were not permitted to copy from text-books at an examination. The following report on the incident appeared in a national daily newspaper:

'UNRULY STUDENTS LATHI-CHARGED AT DURGAPUR

'Police made a mild lathi charge in front of a zone multipurpose school of Durgapur Steel town today to disperse a group of violent student demonstrators. Sixteen persons, all of them students, were arrested by police in this connection.

'It is stated private students appearing in the mathematics paper in the said school became agitated from the very start when they were not allowed to adopt unfair means by the invigilators. The students could not create disturbance during the examination as police were posted near the examination hall.

'As soon as the final bell was given some students (most of them submitted blank papers) came out of the examination hall and started throwing brickbats at the school premises. The students also damaged some furniture and the laboratories of the school. When the situation reached climax police intervened and made a mild lathi charge to disperse the student demonstrators.

'On their way back the students also attacked the buses owned by Durgapur Steel Plant in the township maintenance garage. Some buses were also damaged.

'It may be stated, on the very first day of the school examination about 500 students from the said school went out of the examination hall when their demand for free copying was rejected.'

It was with a feeling of some guilt that I started again along the Grand Trunk Road next morning, now only one hundred miles from Howrah, because I felt I should have visited the steel plants and listened attentively to figures indicating India's progress since the First Five Year plan. Only a few days later, however, I read that the steel mills at Durgapur had lately been making heavy losses.

The results of months of fairly frugal living were mainly to be observed in my clothing. My shoes had been rehabilitated by a cobbler in the square in front of Durgapur station; many attacks on them by indifferent craftsmen had left them lumpy and distended, but they were still comfortable, and I still wear them at weekends. Both my Madras cotton shirts, celebrated for their 'bleeding', had bled freely and long since lost most of their colour. My cotton trousers, the pair I had worn for most of the way between Peshawar and Durgapur, were frayed about the turn-ups and pockets, and clear tracks had been left by repairs along the seams at the seat. My rucksack showed little sign of the extra wear it had received in Pakistan and India, because after fifteen years of hard use there were few ways in which it could acquire any more noticeable markings and tears. Altogether I must have appeared a notably penurious traveller, and yet, incredibly it seemed to me, local rickshaw men still refused to quote me anything less than twice the proper price for a journey.

Out on the Grand Trunk Road I succeeded almost immediately in hitching a ride in a truck bound for Calcutta. I was now well into the rice belt, a patchwork of bare or stubbly mud fields coloured by the occasional green nursery of rice seedlings. The people here were short and dark, and seemed more akin in features to Burmans or Thais than to the Indian of the Punjab, Hariana, Uttar Pradesh or even Bihar. The houses were covered with thatch and were often difficult to see, being nearly hidden in the thick vegetation of bamboos, palms and banana trees that surrounded each village. The air was hot and humid; most men worked in dhothis, and the women, though they wore saris, made little effort to cover their upper bodies.

Occasionally we came upon government check-posts where the traffic was very effectively slowed not by a barrier or a chain across the road, but by two parallel ridges in the tarmac, just three to four inches high, which would probably have broken the chassis of any truck that tried to cross at speed. The Grand Trunk Road was now a broad highway, but it was not as interesting as it had been. One reason was the lack of foot traffic along the road, and want of evidence of any stream of life having passed along the road in the past. I had seen few shrines since entering Bihar, and no signs of the paraos, camping places, that had been a feature of the road through the Punjab and Uttar Pradesh. Thirty-four miles before Howrah a new direct approach road had been built and the truck took this route. I alighted to continue along the Grand Trunk Road, which now meandered as quietly as a country lane past deserted stalls that had been closed when traffic to Calcutta had taken the new route. After some miles the road approached the old townships along the Hooghly river, where some of the earliest European settlements in India had been; Bandel of the Portuguese, Chandernagore of the French, and Serampore, formerly Fredericksnagore, of the Danes, many of their buildings showing the style of architecture common to the country of origin of their early settlers. After Bandel the Grand Trunk Road comes upon hard times; it is pitted with holes and is so narrow that two vehicles can scarcely pass one another.

I rode for some miles in a very crowded bus, designed in the fashion of Bengal buses with no intention of allowing passengers to look at the scenery from the windows, with seats arranged round the edge of the interior so that passengers always look inward and have their view impeded by standing passengers. At dusk I came to Serampore and decided to stay for the night: I was now only thirteen miles from Howrah and I wanted to arrive there in daylight. The Grand Trunk Road through Serampore is a narrow and dirty way with no footpath along the edges for pedestrians, who are forced by traffic against the open gutters. People I questioned were adamant that there was no hotel in Serampore and I was about to go to the station in the hope that it had a waiting room where I could stay for the night when someone asked, in almost reverential tones, whether I was a hitch-hiker. At the hour of need I had been discovered by two students from the local Christian degree college, founder members of a hitch-hiking club in Serampore. I was led away as an honoured guest to the old quarter of the town, where some fine old buildings were memorials of the days when Serampore had been a Danish settlement. The contrast between the shabby environs of the Grand Trunk Road and the spacious mellow buildings by the Hooghly river was sudden and refreshing, as the road and the river are only a few hundred yards apart. The college itself had been founded 150 years earlier by the Baptist missionaries, Carey, Marshman and Ward, who were active in this area for many decades.

The Hooghly was broad and full, and in the early morning, when a thin heat haze already veiled the distant outline of the factories at Barrackpore on the opposite shore, it looked like an inland sea. A few fishermen were stowing their nets on long, slender craft for which the Hooghly is famous, and broad-beamed boats with rudimentary gaff sails were being loaded with cargo from the local jute mills. I would have enjoyed going to Calcutta by boat on this broad river that had carried the first European commerce to East India, but I still had the Grand Trunk Road, which humble though it now was, had brought me from the north-western gate of the subcontinent to the verge of the eastern seaboard. It was still early morning when I set out once more on my way.

A continuous straggle of untidy buildings line the last thirteen miles of the Grand Trunk Road between Serampore and the Botanical Gardens at Howrah. I was now in the overcrowded heart of West Bengal. In Uttar Pradesh I had walked for miles without being questioned, but now I met people even more inquisitive than the people of the Punjab.

When the great girders of Howrah Bridge came into sight I was nearly at the end of the Grand Trunk Road. Barely three miles further on, by Number Three gate of the Botanical Gardens, a red-bereted policeman sheltering from the sun under an umbrella confirmed that I had reached what he called 'the beginning of the Grand Trunk Road'.

Across the Hooghly river lay Calcutta, often called 'the last of the roaring cities'. So much has been written about this, the largest of India's cities, about its chronic social problems, that a visitor might well wonder how a city requiring so much urgent attention can operate at all, let alone operate as vigorously as it does. For Calcutta certainly does not give the impression of being a dying city: it is still a very busy port, a vigorous trading centre, and its people are clever and articulate.

Visitors who arrive in Calcutta from Dum Dum Airport are often appalled by the overcrowded conditions and the signs of poverty on the outskirts of the city, before they even reach the centre of Calcutta. I had arrived by road, however, and had travelled very simply, so perhaps I was less fastidious, and merely recognized that here was an exciting city and a city of character, though I had no doubt that the temper of its crowds could become dangerous.

As Howrah Bridge provides the main approach to Calcutta from the west it carries a very heavy traffic load. The buses were quite as crowded as Calcutta buses are always depicted to be in newsreel features, and the risk involved in clinging to these public transports seemed to me to be far greater than was justified. An alternative transport, the rickshaw, provided an uneasy ride as one has to sit in an elevated position, looking down at the shoulder blades of the man working between the shafts.

Structurally the Calcutta rickshaws are beautiful vehicles, made entirely of wood and perfectly balanced. Most of the rickshaws, it appeared, were hired from entrepreneurs, the normal charge being the equivalent of 10p for a twelve-hour shift; with an overhead like this it was not surprising that the rickshaw man, having brought me to a modest guesthouse behind the great yellow museum building near Chowringhee, should try to augment his fare by offering to take me to girls, 'the finest to be found in all India; Chinese, Japanese, half-caste, European'. After a good-humoured argument about the fare he said he would wait for me outside the guesthouse in the evening in case I changed my mind.

My exploration of Calcutta, however, would have to wait. It was now the end of April; I had two weeks more before I was due to return to London, and like Kim's Lama I pined for 'the Hills and the snow of the Hills'.

I had been lucky on my journey in that I had lost no time through illness on the way. The food and water on the subcontinent had not afflicted me with 'Delhi Belly' or any other of the myriad ailments to which visitors to this part of the world are supposed to be prone.

And the Grand Trunk Road had proved a fortunate choice of route. It had helped to show me lands much stronger and more vigorous than the western world imagines them to be. It had taught me many passwords that would help with future journeys in India, for ritual is an important feature of Indian life and nothing smooths the way better than knowing the form. Most important, the Grand Trunk Road had heightened my interest in the subcontinent and had contrived to show me that I was no stranger there.

And now, one journey done, I could begin another: I had just time enough for a trek in the hills beyond Simla. Now it would be the mela season in the hills; the people of those regions would be dressed in their finery; and the nomads of northern India would be taking their herds to hill pastures. Perhaps I would trek over the hills to Banjar, and continue from there to the Kulu Valley, to stay at the haunted fort in Naggar and climb from there to the Chanderkani meadows, where the snows would now have melted and the mountain flowers would have appeared. The air would be cool in the hills.

It was a pleasant prospect.

'A fair land,' as Kim said, 'a most beautiful land is this of Hind'.